Barry
I hope you enjoy this.
Best regards.
Dan
July 2007

How to Become a
Successful IT Consultant

Dan Remenyi

OXFORD   AMSTERDAM   BOSTON   LONDON   NEW YORK   PARIS
SAN DIEGO   SAN FRANCISCO   SINGAPORE   SYDNEY   TOKYO

Butterworth-Heinemann
An imprint of Elsevier Science
Linacre House, Jordan Hill, Oxford OX2 8DP
200 Wheeler Road, Burlington, MA 01803

First published 2003

British Library Cataloguing in Publication Data
A catalogue record for this book is available from the British Library

ISBN 0 7506 4861 9

The names Apple and IBM and any other commercial organizations mentioned in the
text are the property of the organizations concerned.

For information on all Butterworth-Heinemann publications visit
our website at www.bh.com

Composition by Genesis Typesetting, Rochester, Kent
Printed and bound in Great Britain

Contents

Contents

11   Keep your eye on the ball 118
   11.1 Business cycles 118
   11.2 Fixed priced jobs can be undercosted 120
   11.3 Losing control over cash flow 121
   11.4 The flavour of the month or of the year 121
   11.5 Not understanding the risk facing your
         organization 122
   11.6 The great tax surprise 123
   11.7 Summary and conclusion 124

12   Minding your own business 125
   12.1 Keeping your business going is the real challenge 125
   12.2 Remember why you started your own business 126
   12.3 Money versus quality of life 127
   12.4 Nurturing a sustainable client relationship 129
       12.4.1 IT consultants are offered jobs 129
   12.5 Internal administration 131
       12.5.1 Understanding how your business is
             doing 132
       12.5.2 Income statements 133
       12.5.3 Cash flow statements 134
       12.5.4 Balance sheets 135
       12.5.5 Funds flow statements 138
   12.6 Creating a sustainable working regime 139
       12.6.1 How many hours per week do you
             need to work? 140
       12.6.2 How many weeks a year vacation will
             you take? 140
       12.6.3 How long do you think your working
             life will be, i.e. when do you want to
             retire? 141
       12.6.4 What do you expect to do about your
             pension? 141
       12.6.5 How will you handle being ill? 141
       12.6.6 When do you engage your first
             employee and should this be another
             consultant? 142
       12.6.7 When do you need to look for a
             partner? 142
   12.7 Seeing the opportunities 143
       12.7.1 Growing from strength to strength .. 145
       12.7.2 What the Internet can do for you 146
   12.8 Summary and conclusion 146
   12.9 Checklist 147

Appendices

Computer Weekly Professional Series

There are few professions which require as much continuous updating as that of the IS executive. Not only does the hardware and software scene change relentlessly, but also ideas about the actual management of the IS function are being continuously modified, updated and changed. Thus keeping abreast of what is going on is really a major task.

The Butterworth-Heinemann – *Computer Weekly* Professional Series has been created to assist IS executives keep up to date with the management ideas and issues of which they need to be aware.

One of the key objectives of the series is to reduce the time it takes for leading edge management ideas to move from the academic and consulting environments into the hands of the IT practitioner. Thus this series employs appropriate technology to speed up the publishing process. Where appropriate some books are supported by CD-ROM or by additional information or templates located on the Web.

This series provides IT professionals with an opportunity to build up a bookcase of easily accessible, but detailed information on the important issues that they need to be aware of to successfully perform their jobs.

Aspiring or already established authors are invited to get in touch with me directly if they would like to be published in this series.

Dr Dan Remenyi
Series Editor
dan.remenyi@mcil.co.uk

Preface

The theory of IT consultancy, if in fact there is such a thing as the theory of IT consultancy, would be a dreary subject indeed, and that's not what this book is about at all. This is a very practical book. From this book you can learn about the important issues and the practical steps of how to set up your own IT consultancy business in real no-nonsense, down-to-earth terms.

So this is not a theoretical textbook. It is closer to a 'how to' manual with a focus on how to make a career change happen and of course how to maximize your chances of being a success in your new world of IT consultancy. Understanding the suggestions in this book will help you be one of the success stories and make the most of the computer, information systems and of course the Internet opportunities available.

There are many different ways in which you can follow a career as an IT consultant. There are at least four different levels at which an IT consultant may operate and there are literally scores of different fields of specialization. This book covers the different levels and gives a sample of the different specializations that you can consider. Perhaps you will advise organizations on how the organization can profit from the new technologies and make the most of the changes that are going on all around us now. On the other hand you may become a consultant who takes over the top sales hype and makes real practical sense of it. Perhaps you understand high-level technology and can separate it from unfounded rumour and thus be able to tell management what can actually be achieved and what other organizations are doing. In this way you will turn your knowledge of management, business and technology into business reality.

You could have trained in management or accountancy or could even have come up the ranks as a computer programmer and analyst. By now you will probably have slogged your way up the corporate ladder into a position where some people are beginning to listen to you. The main point is that at your current stage you will be able to help point out to others how to cope with the immense technological changes coming our way.

As an IT consultant you will be a person who has a high degree of competency in the use of IT professionals to achieve business goals. You will be optimistic about the use of IT in business. You will be flexible in your approach. You will have a keen sense of adventure and bags of energy and finally you will be realistic in your view of your business potential.

This book will show you how to make the most of a career in IT consultancy.

Dan Remenyi

Acknowledgements

The subject of becoming a successful IT consultant is one of the most captivating topics and it is one which has had a great attraction for me for many years, even before I decided to jump in the deep end and do it for myself. I was convinced that I had to do this when an old friend pointed out that talking about becoming an IT consultant was no substitute for just going out there and doing it. There is nothing like an old friend for providing insights and giving you a nudge in the right direction.

Of course when I started as a consultant in my early thirties I didn't have the benefit of all the ideas discussed in this book. The ideas described here are the result of experiences over a period of more than 25 years working as a computer salesman, software developer and then consultant, during which I have learned what I know from employers, colleagues, friends and in recent years students with whom I have had the privilege to work. The list of the names of people who have contributed to my thinking is far too long to mention any names but those of them who will read this book will recognize their influence.

However, I would like to mention especially the kind help received from three friends, Michael Stanley, Michael Sherwood-Smith and Richard Waller, all of whom read a draft of this book and gave me very interesting comments.

Finally, the illustrations were drawn by Mark de Lange and these have certainly helped to bring a little fun to what is essentially a serious subject.

My thanks to everyone.

About the author

Dr Dan Remenyi has spent more than 25 years working as a computer consultant, during which he has been primarily concerned with the efficient and effective use of information technology. One of his special areas of interest as an IT consultant is the realization of IT benefits and thus obtaining  the maximum value for money from the organizations' information system's investment and effort. In recent years he has specialized in the area of formulation and implementation of strategic information systems and how to evaluate the performance of these and other systems. He has also worked extensively in the field of information systems project management specializing in the area of project risk identification and management. He has written a number of books in the field of IT management and regularly conducts courses and seminars.

He has worked over the years for many organizations both as a management consultant and as an executive development facilitator in different parts of the world. These organizations include IBM, Barclays Bank, Ernst and Young, FI Group, Caterpillar Division of Barlows, Andersen Consulting, National Health Service in the United Kingdom, Spoornet (the national railroad company of South Africa), Liberty Life Insurance Company, and the Anglo Vaal Mining Corporation.

Dan Remenyi holds a B.Soc.Sc., an MBA and a PhD. He is a Visiting Professor at Trinity College Dublin and an associate member of faculty at Henley Management College in the United Kingdom.

How to use this book

This book offers practical hands-on advice as to how to set up and manage an IT consulting business.

For anyone thinking about going into business as an IT consultant this book is a useful text to read throughout.

For those who have embarked on a career as an IT consultant the book has been designed in such a way that most chapters stand alone as useful texts on specific aspects of the subject.

The appendices contain lists of information, including a large number of website addresses that the author believes will be helpful to the IT consultant. For your convenience these addresses have been posted on the author's website at www.mcil.co.uk.

Consultancy – a major opportunity for IT professionals

1

I no longer believe that organizations can be changed by imposing a model developed elsewhere. So little transfers to, or even inspires, those trying to work at change in their organizations. Second, and much more important, the new physics cogently explains that there is no objective reality out there waiting to reveal its secrets. There are no recipes or formulae, no checklists, or advice that describes 'reality'. There is only what we create through our engagement with others and with events. Nothing really transfers; everything is always new and different and unique to each of us.

Wheatley, M., *Leadership and the New Science*, Berrett-Koeler, San Francisco, 1992, p. 7.

1.1 Consultancy: the opportunity

Not long ago IT consultancy was perceived as a highly exclusive profession. There were a relatively small number of large prestigious IT consulting firms who were the major providers of expert advice and service. In addition there were small firms operating in specialist niches. IT consultancy was seen as an exclusive profession that was really quite difficult to penetrate. You either had to get into one of the big firms or you had to be really quite special, probably with a computer science degree or an MBA or a PhD or maybe all three. IT consultants were seen as being remote and very often they were not perceived as delivering much value to organizations. The old quip that says 'a consultant is someone who borrows your watch so as to tell you the time, then pockets your watch without even a thank you and sends you a big bill for having told you what time it is' was created to politely express a profound dissatisfaction with what many consultants actually had to offer. The watch story is an allegory or metaphor for the fact that the organization often has to educate the consultant in the *ins-and-outs* of the particular business before he or she can be effective. Being called *the consultant* by the corporate team was not necessarily a term of endearment.

Today much of this has changed. There is a different attitude to consultancy and specifically to IT consultancy. To begin with the image of consultants is much more positive than it has ever been before and this is due to a number of reasons. In the first place there are many more IT consultancy organizations now, both big and small. These IT consultancy organizations came about because of the enormous need for advice and skills which was generated by several large waves of computerization over the past 20 years. Corporate requirements for IT have simply rocketed. These massive increases in demand for computers and skills resulted

> **IT expenditure**
> It has been estimated that since the mid-1990s many firms have been spending as much on IT investment as they have been on all other investments together, i.e. IT investment has constituted 50% of total amount invested. Even if this statistic was exaggerated by 100% and IT investment was only 25% of total corporate investment it would be a very impressive number indeed. This enormous appetite for information and information-related services are important drivers of the demand for consulting services.

from first, the Big Bang in the City of London in the mid-1980s; then the arrival of the Internet and the Web starting in the early 1990s following by Dot.Com mania leading up to the end of that decade. There has also been the Y2K issue, which offered great opportunities for business firms to shake out much of their legacy systems. All of these computerization initiatives created massive opportunities for IT consultancies, which were in a position to offer independent advice and provide the necessary skills to make systems work.

1.2 Changes brought by the Internet and the Web

It is sometimes suggested that perhaps the greatest and most long-lived of these waves of demand will turn out to have been the arrival of the Internet and the Web. This created an enormous need and subsequent demand for specialist IT advice and skills. These were required and are still needed, not only by well-established organizations, but also by the thousands of new businesses that were created in order to take advantage of the promise of the great fortunes there were to be made out of the Web. In the case of well-established firms their existing IT departments' capacity was already fairly well committed due to the work needed to supply the routine information systems requirements of their organizations when the Internet and the Web revolution exploded. Many of these IT departments just couldn't take on the extra work. So many of these larger organizations with well-established IT departments had to outsource much of their Web development work leading to more jobs for consultants.

And the thousands of new venture capital funded businesses attracted to the Web, much like a moth to a candle, also needed quality IT advice and skills. It was certainly boom time for IT consultancy.

But as mentioned above the Internet and the Web were not the only drivers of the increase in demand for the advice and skills supplied by IT consultants. The year 2000 problem was solved largely by organizations disposing of their legacy systems and acquiring large Enterprise Resource Planning (ERP) applications such as SAP, Baan, PeopleSoft, JD Edwards to mention only a few. These are large, complex systems, which are in terms of human resources very demanding. ERP applications are not software packages that can be easily and quickly dropped into a business. To obtain real value from this type of system it needs to be tailored for each business environment.

Highly skilled and even more highly paid staff is needed to implement these systems. Some if not many companies are unable to find adequate staffing resources of their own to manage all the different aspects of these challenging new application systems. Where this has occurred these organizations have had to turn to IT consultants for help. This has resulted in demand for a large number of IT consultants of all different types and grades. Much the same sort of situation exists in the data warehousing and data mining areas as well as in the field of Intranet and Extranet development and use.

. . . THIS HAS RESULTED IN DEMAND FOR A LARGE NUMBER OF IT CONSULTANTS . . .

1.3 Consultants plug a gap

So, as IT becomes more and more sophisticated, business firms and other organizations will find it harder and harder to obtain suitable staff and will therefore need to use consultants. This trend is likely to continue into the future with more and more IT consultants being needed to help business firms and other organizations cope with ever increasingly sophisticated application systems.

This huge demand for specialist IT advice and skills brought a flood of new organizations into the market place. Some of these new firms are quite big but many are in fact small operations with only one or a couple of people running the business. The range of IT professional services offered by these firms is quite broad. In the Internet and the Web market segment alone there are dozens of specialist consulting operations related to design, to payment collection, to hosting, to business models, to connecting the front office to the back office to mention only a few.

1.4 A major career option

IT consultancy is now a major career option for a wide range of IT professionals, with the last few years seeing dramatic growth in the number of individuals entering the IT consultancy profession. As described above this has been fuelled by the relatively unforeseen exponential growth in IT expenditure during this period.

NEW ATTITUDES

But the growth in IT expenditure alone has not been the only driver of the interest in IT consultancy. Increasingly IT professionals want to break out of large corporate structures and to try business on their own account for themselves. This new attitude has been fuelled by at least two major economic and social developments:

- Employers' attitudes towards staff and staff attitude toward employers.
- Employers' attitude towards consultants.

There has been a major shift in society's attitude towards jobs. Whereas 20 or 30 years ago large organizations frequently offered long-term career opportunities or maybe even a job for life, today that has changed. One of the best examples of this is the IBM organization. When I joined IBM in 1973 I was told that unless I committed a very grave offence I would not be fired. IBM had a non-firing and non-redundancy policy. If I didn't perform well my pay could be reduced. I was after all a salesman, and I could find myself doing more and more boring jobs – a stationery inventory controller was mentioned. But my livelihood was secure. The firm would be loyal to me. This attitude was prevalent in many large organizations that saw security of employment as one of the major factors that talented people wanted.

THIRTY YEARS LATER THIS HAS ALL BEEN THROWN OVERBOARD

Thirty years later this has all been thrown overboard. Redundancy is a way of life in virtually all organizations, including IBM. There is no longer any question of business firms or other organizations for that matter being loyal to their staff. As a general rule today, if the staff don't shape up they have to ship out. If the business turns down then the staff have to walk – get off the payroll as quickly as possible. And in recent years more than a few people have been made redundant more than once. Furthermore once you have reached the age of 50 for certain and in some cases maybe even 40 it is increasingly hard to find another full-time permanent job. This is the reality of early twenty-first century business life. Furthermore it is difficult to see how business conditions will ever be easy again and that there will again be job security which existed 20 or 30 years ago.

It is indeed not surprising that an increasing number of people want to be in business on their own and this is as true for IT professionals as it is for any other group. The idea of staying in one company for a long time, never mind in the same job for life, is as dead as the proverbial dodo. One of the main reasons is that being self-employed you have the opportunity to spread your income risk by having more than one client. So if, or rather when, you finish with, lose or fall out with one client, hopefully you will have a few others to keep you going.

In the second place many established business firms and other organizations are today more willing to use consultants than they were before. Previously the preferred approach was to have all the human resources in the form of full-time employees or members of staff. However, this old attitude led to head count increases. Today companies are really quite sensitive to the number of people that they employ as head count control is regarded by many to be a particularly important critical success factor. This has led to business firms and other organizations being more prepared to outsource a number of different aspects of their operations. One of the key ways in which firms outsource is to use consultants.[1]

The recent popularization of outsourcing is a very important business development, which has created many consulting opportunities. This change in attitude has occurred because an increasing number of firms have realized that their most rational strategy to human resources is to focus intensely on their core competencies and to outsource any other competencies which are not core and which they may only require from time to time. This approach to business resourcing was well addressed by Charles Handy in his book *The Age of Unreason* when he described the shamrock organization, which is shown here in Figure 1.1.

Figure 1.1
The shamrock model organization resourcing

Note the three leaves in the shamrock model are core competencies, outsourcing and flexible resources. This represents the three principal ways that organizations can acquire resources. According to the model of the shamrock organization businesses will prosper if they focus on developing their core

---

[1] There is another way of looking at the new attitude to outsourcing and consulting. As the business environment becomes more competitive it also becomes more complex and this produces a need for more highly competent and qualified staff who are expensive but not all of whom will be needed on a permanent basis. Therefore it makes very good business sense to buy in these skills only in small short bursts when they are actually needed.

competencies (first leaf) so that in these respects they are operating at world-class performance levels. Any business activity which is not core should be outsourced (second leaf). In some instances this proposition is believed to the extent that it is said that if you don't outsource non-core activities you are actually wasting the business's scarce resources. The question of flexible resources (third leaf) concerns the issue of having available a pool of additional people to help the organization cope during its peak seasons. Thus this part of the shamrock model also supports the notion of outsourcing.

. . . ORGANIZATIONS HAVE BEEN ADAPTING SHAMROCK STRUCTURE . . .

At the same time as organizations have been adapting shamrock structure thinking there has been a realization that the old idea of organizational boundaries is not as useful as it was once thought. Not long ago it was felt that everyone outside the organization, including suppliers, essentially had an adversarial attitude. Fortunately this mind set is on the wane as it is realized that collaboration is far more mutually beneficial.

The result of these trends in the market place and the business world in general is that IT consultancy is today, more than it has ever been before, a major career alternative for the IT professional. IT professionals, ranging from IT departmental managers, to project managers, to IT planners and strategic analysts on the one hand, to web designers and web graphics specialists on the other, can relatively easily move into IT consultancy. Of course whether or not they make a success of this is an entirely different matter.

1.5 Requirements to start

To enter the world of IT consultancy on your own, you will need to have a sought after set of professional skills and competencies. You will need to be quite expert in your own field. There are a considerable number of different areas and industry sectors in which it is possible for you to operate and some of these are described in Chapter 4. You will need to have a set of attitudes and an orientation towards work, which are discussed in Chapter 2. And of course you will need some financial resources, which are discussed in Chapter 3 and again in Chapter 10.

Other than the above there is very little in the way of barriers to entering the IT consulting world. But before you take the plunge into a new career read this book and think carefully if becoming a successful IT consultant is really what you want to do.

1.6 Summary and conclusion

Although the demand for consultants has grown faster in some years than in others, this market, especially for IT consulting, will continue to show growth potentially for some time. As a result this has become a major career opportunity for IT professionals. However, this type of work will not suit everyone and you need to consider carefully if you should give up your job and follow this type of career. The questions put to you at the end of Chapter 2 will help you decide if IT consultancy is really for you.

2

Is IT consulting for you?

Now here, you see, it takes all the running you can do, to keep in the same place. If you want to get somewhere else, you must run at least twice as fast as that!

Lewis Carroll, spoken by The Red Queen in *Through the Looking-Glass*, first published in 1872, Chancellor Press, London, 1982, Ch. 2.

Before you begin to invest too much time and effort, never mind money, in preparing to start your own IT consulting business you need to make a realistic assessment of whether you are likely to be successful in this field and if you are likely to enjoy this new way of making a living.

2.1 Must haves for the IT consultant

Having your own IT consulting business is challenging and once you have set it up it is very demanding to keep it going. You will need a whole range of different types of skills, not to mention the fact that you will have to be an entrepreneur. The attributes of entrepreneurship are spelt out in Chapter 5 and it is really quite important that you can honestly say that you have a substantial entrepreneurial streak in your personality. But in addition to all of this there are four other crucial characteristics that you need to possess and if you don't have them you may as well not begin.

- Optimism
- Flexibility

- Sense of adventure and bags of energy
- Ability to persevere
- Realistic view of your business potential

These are *sine qua nons* to being a consultant and if you don't have them don't do it. Do something else for a living. You have to be an incurable optimist. It is absolutely essential that you always see the bright side of any situation. You have to be very flexible. You need to be flexible in a number of different ways, which I will explain later.

OPTIMISM

2.1.1 Optimism

One of the best ways of illustrating the notion of being an incurable optimist is to recall the old story about the twins and the horse manure. The parents of twins decided to give them a surprise Christmas present of real live ponies. Clearly they could not place the ponies in the children's Christmas stockings or at the end of their beds. Thus the parents decided (for some totally unaccountable reason or reasons) to wrap up a small amount of the ponies' droppings in Christmas paper and put it in the children's Christmas stockings. The first child, on finding a parcel of pony droppings in her Christmas stocking, shouted out: 'Goodness gracious me! Who the devil put horse manure in my stocking? When I find out I will murder them!' The second child, on finding the parcel of pony droppings, screamed with delight, 'Horse manure – I must be getting a pony for Christmas!' In the IT consulting context being an incurable optimist means always seeing a pony even when there is nothing more than horse manure lying around. Another way of looking at this is that to be a consultant it is always

Self-confidence

Besides the question of optimism, flexibility and sense of adventure and bags of energy there is the basic personality issue of having a profound sense of self-confidence. If you don't intrinsically feel self-confident, i.e. if you don't profoundly believe in your own abilities, then IT consultancy will be very difficult for you. IT consultancy will inevitably involve a certain amount of rejection, as not every proposal you present to a prospective client will be accepted. You have to be able to quickly bounce back. Also from time to time you may fall out with clients and this can lead to nasty fights. Thus if you don't have a high degree of self-confidence and a fundamental belief in yourself this will be very painful.

very useful to be able to see a bottle as being half full rather than half empty.

2.1.2 Flexibility

The question of flexibility is a bit more complex. A successful IT consultant will be flexible in several different ways. In the first place there is the type of IT service you plan to offer. It may well be that you are looking for IT strategy assignments and that you are not doing well at finding these. However, as you are looking for this type of work you could encounter organizations needing project management consultancy. Now if you are a reasonably able consultant with a varied background you may well be able to take project management assignments and perform these types of assignments perfectly adequately. This is really a question of your flexibility. I have known IT consultants who have refused to take on work that they were perfectly competent to do because it was not in the field they ideally wanted to be in. Of course the people I have known who have taken this attitude have not succeeded as IT consultants and within 12 or 18 months they were back on the labour market looking for a job.

> **If you're so smart**
> When you first start out as a consultant, be it an IT consultant or a general business consultant, you may find people will say to you 'if you are so smart as to be able to offer advice why then do you not have your own business'. Of course the point is that you do indeed have your own business, which is the business of IT consultancy and which will hopefully provide you with a richly rewarding career both in terms of job satisfaction and income earning capacity.

The next way in which it is important to be flexible is in terms of the way you price your work. It is sometimes quite difficult to get the daily fee rate you are looking for. In such cases you need to be a flexible wheeler-dealer. This means that you have business nous. In practical terms it means that you need to be creative about how you present proposals to clients and how you obtain your rewards. As well as the fee being too low, sometimes you may have to do more than you would like for a particular fee and you need to be able to construct a value proposition for your client and yourself so that you both are on the right side of the equation. There are no simple

STRATEGY ASSIGNMENT

PROJECT MANAGEMENT

FLEXIBILITY

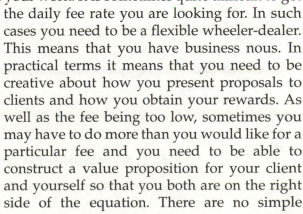

guidelines here. If you are to succeed as an IT consultant you will develop a nose for what you can charge. When you are confident enough you might even be able to say when asked what your fee is that 'Like all consultants you are looking for as big a fee as you can get and that like all successful consultants you will take the fee which the client is comfortable in paying.'

2.1.3 Sense of adventure and bags of energy

The third issue that needs to be faced right upfront is that IT consulting is a relatively insecure way of making a living. There are many IT consultants, all of whom are bidding competitively for assignments. There is of course quite a lot of work around but nonetheless there are plenty of disappointed IT consultants. Many firms employ IT consultants because they do not want to commit to the long-term employment of staff. Therefore IT consulting contracts tend to be relatively short and thus you have to keep your eye out perpetually for new work. The effect of this is that IT consultants often do not know where their next month's revenue will actually come from. This suits some people who are entrepreneurs or risk takers and who like the adventure of continually meeting new people and finding and signing up clients. And of course the more you do this the better at it you will become. But others can find this insecurity devastating and cannot function properly in such an environment. IT consulting is just not suitable for people like this and if you feel that you fall into this category, you should stop now and find another way of making a living.

> **Is there any job security anymore?**
> It used to be thought that consulting was an insecure way of making a living and in some senses it certainly is. But as jobs for life hardly exist anymore and outsourcing, restructuring and merging are the order of the day, perhaps consultancy may not really be as insecure as it was once thought to be. If the security issue bothers you but you still want to take on an IT consultancy career then you could do a risk analysis, which will highlight for you just how much of a risk you are taking.

SENSE OF ADVENTURE

2.1.4 Ability to persevere

An ability to persevere is really all important. Very few start-up IT consultants fall on their feet from day one. It can take months

REALISTIC VIEW OF YOUR BUSINESS POTENTIAL

before the business opportunities begin to arrive. This start-up period can be quite frustrating and you need to be able to retain your sense of confidence and also your sense of humour. It is very important not to give up too soon.

2.1.5 Realistic view of your business potential

Although optimism is the first requirement discussed here and it is perhaps the most important it really does have to be tempered with realism. There is no point in simply imagining that you will be able to sell £100,000 or £150,000 worth of consultancy and be able to grow your business at 20% or 50% or 100% unless you have real evidence to back up such plans. Putting some numbers down on a spreadsheet and doing what-ifs on your prospective IT consulting business without grounding them in real contract is likely to lead to disappointment.

Besides these four crucial issues, before you jump you also need to consider the following.

> **Working hours**
> The average IT consultant is said to work about 60 hours a week with considerable sacrifice to his or her personal life. And sometimes he or she is simply not adequately rewarded for the effort involved. As the IT consultant is intrinsically an optimist there is always the expectation that *things will get better!*

Successful IT consultancy is as much to do with being able to sell and then to get on with your clients as being technically capable. If all your strengths are to do with your knowledge of the technology then maybe you should reconsider IT consultancy as a career.[1] Another issue is that you need to be a self-starter. By this I mean that you need to be self-motivated. You need to be able to drive yourself onwards even when you don't really feel like it. There is also the question of your ability to communicate. To succeed as an IT consultant you need to be a competent communicator, both verbally and of course in writing. And as

---

[1] Delivering benefits to your client organization is what ultimately counts and this can seldom be achieved by just being an outstanding technologist. You obviously have to be completely in command of the technology you are working with but you need a range of other skills as well, as will be explained later in this book.

well as communicating there is the question of being able to keep confidences, which is perhaps just as important. This question of keeping confidences is of course closely aligned to one's values, especially as they relate to one's sense of integrity. Whatever your skill base in starting out as an IT consultant you will find that you will need to continually learn and relearn. Therefore for success as an IT consultant you need to be fully committed to life-long learning. There is no way of getting out of this – as long as you are a consultant, learning has to be one of your most urgent responsibilities to yourself.

One final point, sometimes people say that they want to get into IT consultancy because they are tired of working for a boss. They say that they want the independence of being self-employed. Such people often imagine that as a self-employed IT consultant they will be able to start work at 10 am and finish at 4 pm. When the mood takes them they will indulge in long leisurely lunches. They will be able to take the kids to school and pick them up, take long weekends off whenever the fancy takes them. They will have six or eight weeks' vacation every year. These types of individuals have somehow acquired the notion that it isn't hard work to be self-employed. It is quite puzzling as to precisely where this type of thinking comes from. It is perhaps some misunderstood interpretation of portrayals from nineteenth century literature.

YOU MAY HAVE TO WORK 50, 60 OR EVEN 80 HOUR WEEKS

The reality of being self-employed, especially in the field of IT consultancy, is that it is very, very hard work. Instead of having one boss, each and every one of your clients will in effect be your boss. In addition if you have had to take a loan your bank manager may also hassle you. To make a success of an IT consultancy career you will have to be even more dedicated than you were in your full-time job. You may have to work 50, 60 or even 80 hour weeks. You may have to travel extensively. A client can call you out in the middle of the night – and it's hard to say no. As a consultant once you have said no to a client you can expect not to be asked a second time. IT consulting can be very rewarding indeed, but it is seldom to do with the fact that you are likely to have more leisure time, especially in the short term. You need bags of energy and a will to work. When you are a well-established consultant and have more work than you can cope with then you can think about balancing your work and your leisure.

... PHYSICALLY, INTELLECTUALLY AND EMOTIONALLY DEMANDING

The objective of this chapter is not to put you off or to discourage you in any way from starting up your own IT consulting business. There are loads of great opportunities out there right now if you want to take up the challenge of finding the work and managing it successfully. The objective of this chapter is rather to ensure that you understand some of the really important personal attributes necessary to be a great success in such an endeavour.

IT consultancy is not an easy profession. It is physically, intellectually and emotionally demanding. However, for those who succeed the rewards can be most satisfying. You will see how your efforts help your clients overcome problems; you will observe your clients' businesses prosper; you can enjoy learning and keeping up or increasing your skill base, and sometimes you can even make quite a lot of money. For the right sorts of people IT consulting is a career choice that they should give very serious consideration.

2.2 Summary and conclusion

It is important to think carefully about whether IT consultancy will suit you. It really does not suit everyone. Talk to other IT consultants whom you meet about their working lives and how they cope with the challenges they face. Find out what they like most about their work as well as what they like least. Do the self-test below and then discuss the results with your friends and family. Take as much advice as you can about your options. But always remember if you try IT consultancy and you don't like it or it doesn't work for you it is always possible to get another job.

2.3 Self-test on the characteristics necessary for IT consulting

There are a number of personal characteristics or attributes that you should have if you are likely to succeed as an IT consultant. You will find here 12 of the more obvious personal attributes. It is not intended to be a definitive list but just a rough guide to stimulate your thinking about whether IT consulting is really for you.

Thus if you feel inclined rate yourself on a scale of 1 to 5 on the following personal characteristics, where 1 is low and 5 is high:

		1	2	3	4	5
1	Level of general optimism					
2	Self-starter					
3	Risk taker					
4	Flexibility in work					
5	Wheeler-dealer					
6	Communications ability					
7	Report and proposal writing ability					
8	Listening ability					
9	Keeping confidences					
10	Ability to work hard					
11	Ability to work long hours					
12	Committed to life-long learning					
	Total score					

Figure 2.1 The IT consulting aptitude self-test

Scores and their implications

60   You have all the characteristics you need to make a great success of an IT consulting business of your own. Just go for it. But make sure that you have been really honest with yourself.

50 to 59   Operating a successful IT consultancy business should be well within your reach.

40 to 49   You have a reasonable amount of potential for creating an IT consulting business, but you will need to hone up some of your personal characteristics.

39 or less   Think very hard before you embark on an IT consulting career as you might just find the going very tough.

In general if you scored less than 4 for any of the issues in the IT consulting aptitude self-test you will need to improve. You need to be just excellent in pretty well all these issues if you are going to make it as a successful IT consultant.

If your scores are low on a couple of these attributes but you still want to try being an IT consultant, don't despair. But you will find it helpful to put time and energy into improving the particular attributes.

3

Setting up your IT consultancy business

Even today's most careful students of organisations will readily admit that they lack adequate models to predict corporate success. Recall how widely we celebrated such New Age cultures as People Express, Atari, and Rolm. Ardent supporters include academics, consultants, business journalists, and seasoned executives. Our former enthusiasm becomes a source of embarrassment when we hold ourselves accountable for predictive accuracy.

Pascale, R., *Managing on the Edge*, Penguin Books, London, 1990.

Before beginning to think about how to set up your IT consultancy business you need to have clearly answered for yourself three important questions, which effectively will define your business strategy and focus your activities and which in turn will affect how you set up your new business.

3.1 Three focusing questions

1 Precisely what service is it that you are going to be offering to deliver to your clients?
2 To whom exactly are you going to be offering?
3 Specifically why will anyone want to buy from you?[1]

These three questions are fundamental to all businesses, ranging from the start-up IT consultants to large global multinational businesses, and without a clear view as to how you will address these issues you will not have a business. In fact without being able to convincingly answer these questions you had better not start out on a business venture of your own. The answers you

---

[1] These three questions should be the continuous mantra of every business or at least every entrepreneur. Once you lose sight of these the business's survival is definitely in question.

come up with need to be objective, i.e. not just answers you personally like or your mother-in-law likes.

The first question is the '**what**' of your IT consultancy. The range of services which you could offer as an IT consultant is quite substantial and it includes assisting companies with the selection of hardware, software and personnel. IT consultancy also includes the preparation of systems involving such tasks as project management, risk management, systems testing and commissioning. It could also include staff training, information systems evaluation and advising on the alignment of information systems and corporate strategies.[2] There are many more services you might offer as an IT consultant, and the above mentioned are only a few. The point is that you need to have a clear focus as to what it is you are offering.[3]

The second question is the '**to whom**' of your IT consultancy. The issue of to whom you are offering this service is very important because there are different requirements in different market segments and different propensities to purchase IT consultancy. In the first place although there is a major need among small firms for IT advice, there is in general not much of a market here. The main reason for this is that small firms often do not have the necessary funds to purchase IT consultancy. This is not to say that there is no market for IT consultancy among small firms but it is a limited one and a difficult one in which to succeed. Bigger firms are more likely to buy IT consultancy. Some IT consultants specialize by industry and thus some aim their services at transport firms or hotels or retailers or at municipal councils to name only four possible industry sectors. There is also the question of who it is in the organization that is likely to support the employment of the IT consultant. This will usually be the IT manager[4] or a general manager or a director. The organization's accountant or financial manager or director is also a possible purchaser of IT consultancy.

[2] The term IT consultant is in fact extremely broad and it is often surprising just what activity can be classified under this heading. There is no source of authority to say what is IT consulting and what is not. People just use the language differently.

[3] All businesses have to cope with the dilemma that to succeed they need to be highly focused, while at the same time they need to be sufficiently flexible so that if the market for their products and services changes they can quickly respond and change as well.

[4] It is important always to bear in mind who actually brings the IT consultant into the organization as that person will no doubt be the IT consultant's strongest supporter and friend. If the IT manager did not personally request the assistance of the consultant this can cause the consultant headaches.

The third question is the '**why**' of your IT consultancy, and this is perhaps the most difficult on which to generalize. You will be employed as an IT consultant only if you are able to convince your potential client that you are an expert in your field. You will have to have outstanding references.[5] You will have to be clearly achievement motivated. You will have to be available when the client requires your services. You will have to price yourself competitively. It will be essential that you deliver value for money. You will need to clearly articulate your value proposition to your clients and continuously make sure that they keep this in their minds.

... PRESENT THE IDEAS TO YOUR BANK MANAGER ...

As you can see being an IT consultant is no pushover. In fact in many ways it is actually quite a tall order.

You need to test your views about why you should succeed as an IT consultant in the harsh business world. One way to do this is to present the ideas to your bank manger while asking him or her for a substantial loan to fund your business. By the way, completely on the side, banks very seldom fund a consultancy business as it is thought that by the very nature of business consultancy this type of enterprise should be largely self-funding. This is because if properly managed a business consultancy should not need extensive set-up capital nor should it need much by way of working capital. There is seldom any need for a consultancy business to invest in expensive equipment and there is hardly ever any need for a consultancy to purchase inventories for resale. Banks and other lending institutions are

> **Professional Service Firms**
> Your IT consultancy will be a Professional Service Firm. Professional Service Firms are not regarded as good risks by banks who want the organization to whom they will lend money to have fixed assets or at the very least assets such as inventories. Therefore you will need to fund your IT consultancy in ways other than overdrafts. Fortunately if you are careful you may not need too much money to get started.

---

[5] The question of references is in fact a thorny one. Not every potential IT consultant will be able to leave his or her firm with a good reference. Sometimes it's just the chemistry which hasn't worked and the individual can be forced to leave under a cloud. On the other hand a completely incompetent individual can negotiate a 'good' reference as part of a severance package. If you can't obtain an outstanding reference from your employer you will need to find other people who will have good things to say about you and who will put those words in writing.

really interested in funding only these types of physical assets. But it is certainly an essential experience for anyone who is thinking of setting up an IT consultancy business to talk to his or her bank manager.

But back to business strategy – these three questions are the underpinning of the business strategy from which the business plan is created. You need to develop a business plan as part of the process of setting up your IT consulting business. If you get your strategy wrong at this stage then your subsequent planning will be based on false premises and you may very well not succeed.

Having decided on your business strategy there are many different ways in which you may set yourself up as an IT consultant. There is no right or wrong way and the actual route you eventually choose will be entirely dependent on your personal circumstances and preferences. It is important to realize that you will be creating your own business and that you will be running the show in the way that you want to and that subject to keeping your clients satisfied you would have quite a lot of latitude as to how you can actually do this.

Here are some of the issues you need to consider right at the very outset of your venture into business.

3.2 Form of business

Are you going to be a sole trader working by yourself or will you start out with a business partner?

There are many pros and cons to being either entirely on your own as opposed to having a business partner from the outset. The main issue is that being entirely on your own means that you have very definite restrictions in that you may not have someone to help with the large variety of things that need to be attended to when you start up. Also there is always the issue that when you first begin to work for yourself you may well miss the company of your former colleagues. In simple terms being entirely on your own is often perceived as being quite lonely and if you have a business partner this feeling may be alleviated. A business partner can have a number of important advantages including providing a sounding board for ideas and of course will bring his or her business contacts and additional funds for the business. It is also true that frequently two minds are better or at

. . . WILL YOU START OUT WITH A BUSINESS PARTNER?

least can be more creative than one. However, it is worth pointing out that there is a risk associated with having a partner. In law each partner can be jointly and severally responsible for all the debts of the partnership. Thus if your partner were to engage in an extravagant binge and your business was to go broke you might have to pick up the whole bill if your erstwhile partner had no money of his or her own to contribute to paying the debts of the business. Also partners do sometimes fall out and this can lead to very unpleasant situations.

A variation of having a partner is for the IT consultant to approach an already established firm of consultants in another field such as marketing, finance or general management and suggest that this organization set up an IT consulting operation with you using their base of clients, etc. Accountants or lawyers are also possibilities for such an arrangement. Working with an already established business whereby the IT consultant uses his or her skills to develop a new market that will be shared by himself and the already established business is sometimes referred to as being in a strategic alliance. However, it is important to note that there is more to a strategic alliance than simply having a commission sales agreement with another well-established business. It is worth noting that these so-called strategic alliances frequently don't last very long, but they can be quite a reasonable way of starting out in the consultancy business.

However, having any sort of a business partner does not suit everyone and the rate of business partnership failure, although not officially published, will be at least as high as marriage failure and it can be a difficult, traumatic and expensive exercise to dissolve a business partnership. Having a bad or poor partner would certainly be much worse than having no partner at all.

Thus the question of whether you begin your business venture being either entirely on your own or having a business partner deserves considerable reflection and discussion before taking the plunge. It is probably true for most people that if they can get going without a business partner they will be better off. It is always possible to take a partner later if the need is really there.

3.3 To be or not to be a company

Are you going to operate as a limited liability company?

There are many financial, risk and tax implications to the decision as to whether you decide to be a limited liability

... RESPONSIBLE FOR ALL THE DEBTS ...

company or just trade (in this case act as a consultant) in your own name or private capacity. Detailed financial and tax advice needs to be acquired from a qualified person, normally a chartered accountant or a lawyer. It is important not to rely only on hearsay advice as how you set yourself up will have implications for you for a very long time.

A key issue that may be addressed here is that of risk. A limited liability company means that if your business fails then you will not be personally responsible for all the debts the business may have run up while it was in the process of failing. This is in contrast to the situation where, if you are trading in your own name or private capacity and your business goes bust, then you will have to pay back every penny that you owe. When a business, which is owned by an individual in his or her own name or private capacity, goes bust the creditors may take just about everything which he or she owns and sell it to repay some of the businesses debts. This can include the family home and most of its contents. Limited liability can protect the start-up entrepreneur against such a catastrophic business failure and thus if prudently used may reduce the risk.

The first few weeks

It you set up a new office and start your IT consultancy as a limited liability company you may find that the first few weeks of your new business life will be taken up with tedious administrative details. This will involve buying your company, appointing accountants, finding an office to rent, leasing equipment, registering for tax, etc. Of course you can outsource this to some extent but you can't just ignore these issues. So you have to put time and energy aside to deal with these details and don't expect to be doing billable work immediately.

Limited liability is indeed a great asset, but it doesn't always offer quite as much protection as it seems to. In the first place there are various responsibilities that the director of a limited liability company has to comply with and if he or she fails to do this, the limited liability may be impacted. There is also the fact that when it comes to borrowing money or even obtaining a large line of credit from a supplier, small company directors are frequently asked to sign a personal guarantee for the amount involved. Signing such a guarantee is effectively waiving the benefit of the limited liability company because if anything goes wrong with the business the director who has signed the guarantee will have to pay up from his or her own resources.

In general it is usually thought that there is much benefit in operating the business as a limited liability company. Such a company may be established quickly by purchasing one 'off the shelf' from an accountant or a lawyer. It will usually come with a made-up name,[6] which has been used for the sake of having any old name to begin with. You can then change the name to something that suits yourself. The set-up costs involved here need not be great, but there is an additional ongoing cost in having a limited liability company.[7] Again if you have a successful business these amounts of money will not be a material consideration.

Having decided on the vehicle in which you are going to do business the next issue is to calculate your financial budget. This involves you in deciding a number of issues including:

1 How much money do you need to start up your IT consulting business?
2 What do you think your first year's or perhaps your first few years' turnover will be?
3 What do you think your ongoing fixed costs will be?
4 What do you think your ongoing variable costs will be?
5 How much cash will you have or do you need?

3.4 The awkward question of capital

How much money do you need to start up your IT consulting business?

First, there is not much point in planning, and especially budgeting, too far ahead. Don't waste your time producing spreadsheets showing how you will do five years ahead. When you start out on the journey of having your own IT consultancy you will not be able to anticipate all the challenges and opportunities that will come your way. It is clear that one of the most important factors in any business success, but especially IT consultancy success, is being able to be flexible. So you may

[6] Lawyers and accountants who specialize in setting up companies sometimes invent names like Disklore or Disklike or Herefor or Justdoor in order to have some temporary name which the Registrar of Companies will accept. When these companies are actually activated their name is usually changed to something meaningful to the people who are running it.
[7] These ongoing costs are mainly to do with annual returns to the Companies Office and if you grow beyond a certain size your company will need to be formally audited.

have to rewrite your financial budget a number of times even in your first year.

The amount of capital that you will need to set up your IT consultancy business may not be substantial and the actual sum involved will depend largely upon your ability to quickly find clients and earn income from them. Some IT consultants go on their own only when they have a client already signed up or nearly signed up. In such a case you may not need a lot of money, although this will ultimately depend on how quickly your clients actually pay your fees. Slow paying clients usually mean that a lot of working capital is needed and this is a major problem for all small businesses and the issue of when payment for services is actually due needs to be addressed right upfront.

> **Get the business going**
> A few years ago two prize winning MBA students decided not to follow the corporate career track but to set up on their own as IT consultants. To this end they set about developing a strategic plan. They commissioned market research. This was followed up by financial projections and cash flow forecasts. They then undertook a major service development exercise. Then they found premises and equipped their office and bought company cars. All this took up three months. Then they started looking for business. This of course was much more difficult than they thought and within six months of setting themselves up they were both in full-time employment with a big bill to pay for playing at setting up a business.

Besides finding your own income there are several reasons why you may need some start-up capital. You may have to replace a company car if you previously had one; you may need a bigger and better computer at home; you may need additional telephone lines and a mobile phone, etc.[8] But all of this equipment may be obtained by using a leasing company without incurring capital expenditure. Of course, leasing is inclined to be an expensive way of funding your business, and it is certainly always more expensive than having your own money and buying the equipment outright. But when money is in short supply leasing may be the answer. By the way, the other disadvantage of leasing is that you will incur fixed monthly payments, which you will have to meet

---

[8] If you can get yourself registered for VAT quickly then you will be able to get back from the VAT authorities all the tax that you will have paid on these capital purchases. This is irrespective of whether or not you are a limited liability company or simply trading on your own. However, the VAT authorities need convincing that you are about to become a serious business before they will allow you to be VAT registered and this can take a little time. It is often worth trying to get VAT registered quickly.

before you can draw any money from the business for yourself.

If you are not able to line up a client to start work with as soon as you leave your old job, then in addition to the money you need to equip yourself you will also have to have sufficient financial resources to sustain yourself until you begin to earn an income from your business. Of course you may also need some money to be spent specifically on marketing. You may wish to put an advertisement in an industry newspaper or professional journal. However, most start-up IT consultants don't do this type of promotion as it's expensive and its effectiveness is questionable. Start-up IT consultants usually market themselves by getting on the telephone and informing anyone who will listen to them that they are in business. This will only cost you your time and your telephone bill. Printing a stylish business card and having an attractive letterhead designed are also part of the cost of marketing your IT consultancy business as is the creation of a website which will explain who you are and what you have to offer. But all of this together will probably only come to a fraction of the cost of purchasing an advertisement in industry newspaper or professional journal.

THE ACTUAL AMOUNT NEEDED WILL DEPEND ON HOW GOOD YOUR BUSINESS STRATEGY IS . . .

There are no general rules as to how big a financial reserve you should have when setting up your business. Some individuals would feel quite comfortable if they had three months' living expenses in the bank when they start the adventure of going on their own. Others would say that three months is not enough and they would want to have secured enough money for a year. The actual amount needed will depend upon how good your business strategy is and how well you execute it. However, do bear in mind that it is perhaps sensible to have whatever sum you think you need available to you in cash or some other financial instrument, which is similar to cash. Having the money in shares on the stock exchange is not the same thing because when you come to cash them in they may not be worth as much as you think.

3.5 A financial forecast

What do you think your first year's or perhaps your first few years' turnover will be?

Estimating your turnover is always very difficult for start-up IT consultants. Even if you begin with a contract it may not last as long as you think. If you go out on your own cold you may be faced with three or six months' canvassing for business before you land a first contract. There are a lot of variables involved here including how much you will be able to spend on advertising or promotion and of course how much you intend to ask as the daily rate for your services.

As an IT consultant your daily charge-out rate will always be determined by how much your clients are prepared to pay and this is referred to as the market rate or what the market will bear. If you are selling very general skills then the market rate will probably be rather low, but if you have specialist and sought after skills then you will be able to ask a much higher fee.[9] It is also worth remembering that most IT consultants do not have one charge-out fee rate, but have several and the one in use will depend on the client they are working for and the length of the job. The charge-out rate on longer jobs is often substantially discounted.

> **The value of your services**
> Economists say that there are two ways of thinking about value. The first is to consider that there is value in use and the second way is to think about value in exchange. The easier of these two concepts is value in exchange, which says that the value of anything is the amount of money for which it changes hands and market forces establish this figure. At the end of the day this is probably the way that your fee rate will be established. Value in use on the other hand is about the positive things you will do for the organization which will allow them to perceive that you have made a real contribution to solving their problem and that you have personally been value for money.

Whatever your circumstances it is useful to perform some analysis on your expected or desired earnings and to think about what your charge-out rate needs to be. Also consider if the demand for your services is likely to be constant throughout the year, or if there is likely to be some sort of cycle in the demand. If there is a possible cyclical effect on the business you are expecting to acquire, then you will have to plan your cash flow even more carefully.

Assuming that you want to be a fairly well-remunerated IT consultant in the short term you may have a target gross income of-say, £100,000. Having established this figure you then need to work out how many days a year you expect to be able to invoice out your services to your clients. If you are an IT consultant working on your own the number of days that you may be able to

---

[9] It is not possible to be specific about fee rates, but a low fee for an IT consultant might be in the order of £300 to £400 per day, while a high fee could be £2,000 to £4,000 per day.

Low fee consultancy

Some of the most successful IT consultants I know operate on really low fees. They do this on the basis that they know if they charge a small amount they will be offered long-term assignments. The type of work they do is usually but not exclusively related to project management or to IT training course development. In this case they are acting much like contractors which suits their particular personalities.

invoice could be quite limited. For example, if you work on a 48 week year – this means that you intend to take four weeks a year holiday, which may be a bit too much in the early years of setting up your own business – and you take an average of one day a week for marketing your services and one day a week for keeping yourself up to date, you would find that you have only 144 days a year to sell. If this is your approach then to invoice out £100,000 per year you will have to achieve an average daily billing rate of £700. On the other hand if you take on a long-term contract and you feel that you do not need the one day a week to keep up to date you could have as much as 192 days a year to sell and thus invoice. Then again, with a long-term contract where you feel that you also do not need the marketing time and you will be able to stay up to date by reading at the weekends, you could have as much as 240 days to sell. This means that to gross £100,000 per year, your average daily billing rate need only be a little more than £400. By the way, if your ambition is to gross £200,000 or £300,000 just double or triple the figures discussed here. But of course you had better be realistic about what is achievable if you don't want to be disappointed.

. . . YOU HAD BETTER BE REALISTIC . . .

However, always remember no matter how you calculate these figures what really matters is how much the client will pay and you need to be prepared to accept a reduced fee for a longer job. It is always useful to know what other IT consultants are charging for similar services to those you are offering. You should always keep this type of benchmark in mind because charge-out fee rates can go down in times of recession and you need to make quite sure that you are not out of line.

Having considered what gross turnover or revenue might possibly be for your first year it is useful to think about how this might grow or develop over the next few years. However, the watchword here is to be flexible and don't think that having a revenue plan guarantees that your business will turn out the way you expect or hope. Always be prepared to tear up your plans and rethink if you find that the market is not responding in the way that you thought it would. Only fleet-of-foot opportunists survive in the world of IT consultancy and it is quite probable that you will have to reinvent yourself several times in the first few years of your being in business.[10]

3.6 Fixed costs

What do you think your ongoing fixed costs will be?

FIXED COSTS

Having considered the initial once-off start-up costs and the revenue side of the income equation it is then necessary to carefully examine the likely ongoing costs of running your business.

These ongoing costs can be considered under two main headings. The first of these are fixed overhead costs which you will have to meet no matter what else happens and the second are variable expenses which will fluctuate depending on the type of work you are actually doing.

As an IT consultant you may be fortunate enough to have only a small amount of fixed overhead costs especially if you first set yourself up in a small way. On the other hand if you want to start your business with a big splash you may need a lot of money.

The main fixed overhead costs you are likely to face are your salary, your rent, your business travel, your equipment costs and sundry other professional costs. As a general rule the lower the overhead costs the better. This rule is true for big and small businesses as well as for start-up operations or for those businesses that have been in existence for years.

It is often the case that in the first few months of operating his or her own IT consultancy it is necessary for the start-up

---

[10] There is a very delicate path to be followed here, which is truly the bane of all consultants' existence. If you chop and change too much you will not succeed because it takes time for you to sort out what you are really doing and what you can really offer the market. It also needs time for any businesses to develop. Therefore perseverance is a critical success factor. On the other hand many start-up businesses just don't begin life with a viable idea and the only way that the entrepreneur will keep going is to pick up a new or better idea and run with it. Perhaps knowing when to hold the idea and when to fold the poor idea is the ultimate difference between winners and losers. This is the same advice that is given to poker players in the song 'you have to know when to hold them and you have to know when to fold them'.

entrepreneur to be flexible in terms of how much salary is taken from the business. If clients are paying good fees then there is no reason why attractive salaries cannot be taken. On the other hand if the business is slow to start then the entrepreneur may need to hold back in paying him or herself and reserve whatever capital he or she may have. This is a very personal issue and depends upon the inclination and expectation of the individuals concerned. But in many cases some sort of salary will need to be budgeted for right from the start of the business.

The second ongoing cost issue is the office rent. This is an especially important issue as rent can be a considerable expense especially in the early months or in fact years of a business.

Some IT consulting businesses may need to acquire a considerable office area and these offices may have to be in an expensive part of town adjacent to clients or prospective clients. On the other hand other IT consultants can actually have their offices anywhere. In fact they can sometimes work from their study or spare bedroom at home. It is becoming increasingly acceptable for IT consultants to work from home and one of the main limitations is the availability for the extra room in the house and the necessary peace and quiet required to get on with the work involved. A successful IT consultant will probably spend a considerable amount of time on his or her clients' premises so the need for an office is largely to do with a place to be when the consultant is not engaged in billable work.

If it is not thought to be appropriate to work from home then there are a large variety of office facilities that are specifically aimed at small start-up businesses. These are office and administrative sharing arrangements and a small amount of space and message taking capability can be acquired for a modest amount of money. Sometimes these office facilities will also offer administrative, secretarial and bookkeeping services. Do not underestimate the importance of this type of service for if you do not keep the records and other legal documents of the business in good order you will soon find yourself in difficulty with a number of government agencies. An administrative mistake, which some small start-up businesses sometimes make, is not to take proper care of the monies which they have invoiced for VAT. Monies invoiced and received for VAT do not belong to the business, as these amounts have to be regularly paid to the government. Spending this money and not having it available when it is due can lead to very severe consequences, including having to suspend one's business activities while one serves a period of time at the Government's convenience in order to square one's debt to society.[11] Administration is always a fixed non-discretionary cost, which will have to be paid each and every month.

In negotiating any office arrangements be careful about the duration of the contract you are asked to sign. Office leases can be very long. You probably should avoid signing up for 5 or 10 years. Office and administrative sharing arrangements are usually short term but there may be a requirement to give three months' notice when you decide to leave. Always look at the fine print of such leasing agreements.

If you have reasonable keyboard or typing skills you will not need secretarial support. However, if you are not skilled in this regard then you should identify a local person who will be able to produce proposals and reports when you require them. This can usually be arranged on a relatively casual basis and be paid for on an hourly rate.

As a general rule the closer your office is to your home the more convenient you will find it.

In the early weeks and months of your IT consulting business you may need to personally call on a large number of potential clients. Sometimes this can involve considerable travel costs and even overnight accommodation, and depending on where you are based and where your potential clients are this travel activity can be quite expensive. It is nearly always better to find business close to home but sometimes this will just not be possible. The amount of speculative travel may reduce once the business is up and running, but in any case it will probably be funded from ongoing revenue. In this category of cost you will also want to budget for a motor car. All these travel costs need to be carefully budgeted.

With regards to equipment costs these may be minimal especially if the necessary car, computer, fax, photocopier, mobile phone,[12] etc. can be purchased at the outset. On the other

[11] Start-up businesses can find the VAT they receive a very useful contributor to their cash flow. In effect you can see VAT, which you receive, from your clients as a sort of borrowing from the Government until your VAT payment date arrives. However, it is normally a very short-term loan as it has to be paid on the due date. If you can't pay your VAT you are likely to be in very serious trouble.

[12] By the way, for an IT consultant setting him or herself up in business on a tight budget there is a second-hand market for all this type of equipment which can substantially reduce the outlay. For most purposes this sort of equipment will be perfectly adequate and can save a lot of money.

hand if all these are leased, and especially if a company car is leased, then these charges could be substantial. Like the rent, these costs will be fixed and need paying each and every month.

Sundry other professional costs are intended to catch all items which will include such expenses as stationery and business cards, insurance, secretarial and administration costs, professional society membership, purchase of books, fees to attend courses to mention only a few items. In total these should be relatively small but nonetheless need to be budgeted.

On the question of insurance you need to decide if you need professional indemnity insurance. Professional indemnity insurance covers you for the risk of your making a serious mistake and being sued because of the consequences. Some IT consultants feel that the cost of this type of insurance is worth the peace of mind it can provide.

The above costs cover all the major categories of ongoing fixed overhead costs that most start-up IT consultants will need to consider.

3.7 Variable costs

What do you think your ongoing variable costs will be?

VARIABLE COSTS

The next task is to consider the issue of variable costs.

From an IT consultant's point of view there are relatively few variable costs that will not be recharged to the client. Many consultants will ensure that their travel and accommodation costs while working for the client are directly rechargeable back to the client. But this is not always the case. Sometimes travel and accommodation costs have to be absorbed by the consultant and if this is the case these costs need careful budgeting to ensure the job is adequately profitable.

Remember that you may be accustomed to travelling business class or full economy, and staying in top class hotels, but that travel and accommodation can be bought for much less if you travel economy or with, for example, discount airlines, etc.

Sometimes the IT consultant will need to produce a report and a number of different types of costs may be associated with this.

These costs might include market research, data analysis, typesetting and reproduction. Like travel and accommodation costs these costs may be directly rechargeable back to the client; on the other hand they may not and this should be clearly established at the commencement of the job.

Bringing the start-up costs together with the revenue plan and the ongoing costs will provide you with a financial budget, which will be an important tool and a guide to you in deciding how to manage your fledgling business. Your next step will be to convert this financial budget into a cash flow plan.

3.8 Cash flow

How much cash will you have or do you need?

The cash flow plan is built up from the data that is used for the financial budget, but as well as estimating what things will cost and how much you will earn, you also need to take into account exactly when you will be paid and when you will have to pay your own bills. By producing the cash flow plan you will know exactly how much cash you will need to borrow or how much extra cash you will have on hand. This is especially useful in the early months of your business when your IT consulting venture is being tried out. The amount of money that you will need to borrow and the salary you are sacrificing by having given up your previous job are effectively the amount of personal risk you are taking on by setting up your own IT consulting business.

3.9 What can the Internet do for you?

The Internet can now play a role in just about every aspect of our lives and setting up your IT consultancy business is no exception.

In the first place the Internet is a magnificent directory. So you will be able to use it to find all sorts of suppliers from business cards to motor cars to computer equipment to accounting services. This will be useful especially to help you compare terms and conditions being offered.

In its capacity as a directory the Internet will also contain details of IT consultancy offers. So you can easily see what the competition is saying and offering. This can give you ideas of how to pitch your market offering.

WHAT CAN THE INTERNET DO FOR YOU?

The Internet will also provide news and information about the IT business from which you can obtain ideas about which firms might be useful prospects for you to contact.

Once you have set up your business you will probably want to have a website for your IT consultancy business. You need to give a lot of thought as to how you present yourself on the Web and you need to take into account that fact that a website can produce a lot of enquiries that may not lead to any business.[13] So from a business assignment acquisition point of view do not have too great an expectation of what the Web can do for you. Some consulting work may well come to you through your website but don't count on it. It is certainly important to have a Web presence but at least in the early days of your IT consulting business you should not put too much reliance on it to produce business.

3.10 Getting going

Setting up your IT consulting business does take time. If everything works well then you can make all the arrangements you will need in a few days or perhaps a week, but on the other hand it could easily take several weeks. So give yourself enough time. It isn't necessarily a good idea to have to share your attention between setting up your business and doing your first IT consulting job, although this has been the way many people have started their business. There is enough stress in either of these two activities never mind both together.

Making all the arrangements described in this chapter does not mean that you have a business. Only when you have a satisfied client who has paid your fees do you really have yourself a business at all. Never lose sight of this fundamental fact.

3.11 Summary and conclusion

There are actually two types of work required in setting up your IT consultancy business. The first of these is the thinking through of all the strategic issues including how you will target your business and what sort of strategic alliances you will be looking for. The second is the work required to actually set up the physical arrangements such as the office and the book-keeping, etc.

[13] One example of this is the fact that offering IT courses and conferences on the Web led to numerous enquiries from individuals in far-away countries who really had no interest in attending these events but who had the time to attempt to engage in dialogue with the course providers.

Take time to get all this right, as you really don't want to start your business off on a bad footing. The time needed to fix problems arising out of not setting yourself up correctly can often be much greater than the time needed to do it right in the first place.

3.12 Checklist

Things to think about and do when setting up your IT consultancy

1 Exactly what IT consultancy service you intend to offer and who is your target market and why they will buy from you.

2 Decide if you are going to be entirely on your own or be in some sort of partnership or strategic alliance. If the latter, sort out the responsibilities and the sharing of costs and revenue with your partner or strategic ally before you proceed any further. Make sure all these details are clearly understood and written down.

3 If you decide that you want to work as a limited liability company then have your accountant or lawyer set up a company for you. Buy a company off the shelf and then change its name.

4 Make sure you identify who will look after your administration including your billing, payments, your returns to the Companies Office and the VAT office.

5 If you don't type or use a word processing package confidently then identify who will produce your proposals and your reports.

6 Make a list of the hardware and software you will need. A motor car, a computer, a mobile phone, a photocopier, etc.? A word processing package, a graphics or presentation creation package, a spreadsheet, etc.?

7 Decide what the cost of this equipment will be and if you can afford to buy it all new or if you need to look for second-hand gear or whether you need leasing finance. Be clear in your mind that leasing is very expensive and avoid this if you can.

8 Are you going to rent office space or are you able to work from home?

9 Work out how much your charge-out rate will be. Find out what other IT consultants are charging for similar services. Remember that ultimately your clients will decide how much they will pay you.

10 Write some terms and conditions that you can show your clients. These need to include when you expect to be paid for your services.

11 Make a list of your fixed ongoing costs. The lower the fixed costs the more successful your business is likely to be. Remember that you may have to be flexible about how much salary you can take from the business.

12 Think about the variable costs you are likely to face.

13 Use your estimates of capital costs, revenue and ongoing costs to produce a cash flow plan.

14 Don't expect to be able to set up your business in an afternoon.

15 It is worth taking time to set up your IT consultancy business well because if you do this correctly it will prevent hassles and save you time in the future.

16 Never kid yourself! There will be complications at every stage, and revenue remains, even for you, so very different from profit.

4

The consultancy options

It is an extraordinary era in which we live. It is altogether new. The world has seen nothing like it before. I will not pretend, nobody can pretend, to discern the end. But everyone knows that the age is remarkable for scientific research . . . The ancients saw nothing like it. The moderns have seen nothing like it till the present generation.

Daniel Webster, 1847, cited in *The Great Reckoning* Davidson, J. and Rees-Mogg, W. Sidgwick & Jackson, London, 1993.

There is a very wide variety of IT consultancy options and opportunities available to you and it is important that you have a clear picture of where you are focusing your attention. There are decisions to be made about areas of IT consulting competencies as well as industry specialization. In addition there is also the question of the orientation of the consulting work.

It is really important not to chop and change too much so you have to think carefully about these issues before you start. Of course this does not mean that you should not be flexible but it is probably quite important not to change frivolously.

4.1 Core competence or expertise

To begin with it is important to remember that an IT consultant is an expert in a specific aspect of how to make optimal use of the organizations' investment in computer and telecommunications technology. It is important to emphasize that the consultant is someone who is highly competent and has in-depth knowledge and experience that can be brought to the aid of an organization when it has a specific problem. It is therefore essential that you select the specific area in which you want to work and that you focus on being able to offer high quality advice and deliver real value for money when working in this arena. This will be your area of core competence.

Keeping your focus on your core competence or expertise is really quite essential for two main reasons. The first is that it is difficult enough to acquire and maintain a high level of expertise in one specific area. The second reason is that if you attempt to be expert in several areas your credibility may be impacted and you may well be seen as a low-level jack-of-all-trades.[1] In the IT consulting world there is no advantage in being a jack-of-all-trades and there is the real danger that no one will perceive you as adequately qualified to do any consulting job.

As IT professionals sometimes have a reasonably wide range of skills it's important to spend some time thinking about the area you will present yourself as expert in. It is important that you are quite confident that you can hold your own in this field. If you are shown not to be competent then you will certainly lose face if not your client as well.

4.2 Flexibility is key

However, you will have noted from Chapter 2 that as well as being focused you also sometimes need to be flexible to the extent of taking work that may not be directly in your field of greatest competence or expertise. You may therefore have a few areas that you can work in kept in reserve[2] in case you are not successful in finding the type of work you would really like. When this happens and you need to move into an area of secondary competence you then need to make quite sure that you quickly become expert in this area too.

---

[1] There is an old joke sometimes told about consultants and the ranges of assignments they are often prepared to undertake. The story goes that a consultant is a person who can read a book and who is prepared to travel. The inference is that the consultant will become an expert in the field required by the client by reading the book on the way to the job.

[2] What type of work you might be able to keep in reserve will obviously depend upon your background. A number of prospective IT consultants may well have project management skills which they don't especially want to offer but on which they could fall back on, for example. Some prospective IT consultants may actually be able to develop code in some sort after language which might be another source of income if the original plan does not work out as expected.

It is a good idea to identify what exactly your areas of core and secondary competence are. The Consultancy Opportunity Matrix (section 4.4) may be helpful to you in so doing.

As well as the core competency issue itself you may well want to decide into which industries you should market your competency. You may well have a preferred industry and one or two other secondary industries as well.[3]

With regards to the question of the orientation of the consulting work it is often said that there are many levels of consulting practices. Here are five possible levels which are worth considering:

- Creative or lateral thinking assignments
- Experiences-based assignments
- Procedural assignments
- Hands-on assignments
- Responsibility assignments

4.2.1 Creative or lateral thinking assignments

Creative or lateral thinking assignments are about offering your client advice that is based on your ability to brainstorm and to come up with new and creative ideas for solutions to problems or ways of taking advantage of opportunities. Such assignments may involve a degree of research, but the focal point of this type of work is not so much the research itself, but the creative interpretation of the findings of the research. With this type of work imagination plays as big – if not bigger – role than experience. Examples of this type of work include reformulating IT strategies and developing IT sourcing policies. Assignments where you are invited to facilitate discussion or debate among boards of directors would also fall under this category of consulting work.

4.2.2 Experiences-based assignments

Experiences-based assignments call upon the many years of practical work which the consultant can draw on. These types of assignments are not for the young man or woman, but rather for

---

[3] Although IT skills often transcend industry boundaries you may have spent a lot of time in the travel industry, for example, and want to continue working in that sort of environment.

those who have been working in the field for, say, 10 or 20 years. They do not require such a high degree of creativity, but rather depend on technical competence tempered by previous experiences. Examples of this type of work include setting up security procedures and developing guidelines for staff selection.

4.2.3 Procedural assignments

Procedural assignments rely on the consultant being technically competent. Here the issue is simply knowledge of the subject matter. Consultants working in this area or mode need not be especially creative. In fact creativity might in some circumstances be a drawback. Neither will the consultant require a vast reservoir of experience. The emphasis here is on having the particular skill set required to solve a relatively limited or focused problem. Examples of this type of work include introducing project management techniques and establishing standards for systems documentation.

4.2.4 Hands-on assignments

Hands-on assignments involve the actual doing of work. In this type of assignment the consultant actually undertakes the management of an IT project or contracts to write a piece of software required to solve the problem. It is sometimes argued that hands-on assignments should not really be regarded as consultancy, but that this type of work comes under the heading of contracting. Clearly there is a substantial grey area between consulting and contracting assignments and the language used to describe the work is perhaps irrelevant. Examples of this type of work include designing an IT architecture and writing an invitation to tender.

4.2.5 Responsibility assignments

The responsibility assignment may take two different forms, the first being more positive while the second is really quite negative. IT consultants are sometimes employed to basically hold the organization's hand while it makes an important decision. This can take many forms, for example helping the firm choose a specific vendor or making a senior appointment to a top IT job. IT consultants are also often asked to read and comment on the organization's IT strategy to see if any important elements have been left out or need enhancement. This type of assignment has the subtext that if a mistake is made

... THE IT CONSULTANT WILL BEAR SOME OF THE
RESPONSIBILITY

then the IT consultant will bear some of the responsibility. Or putting it an other way the corporate executive will not be wholly responsible. If things go wrong some of the blame can be placed on the consultant.

The second type of responsibility assignment occurs when the organization has a very unpopular and difficult decision to take. In such a case consultants are invited to assist with this decision. Sometimes the organization may have already decided what to do and they simply await the consultant's confirmation of the unpopular course of action. Here the management can point to the consultants and say that the unpopular course of action was recommended by the consultants. This rather cynical use of consultants can backfire sometimes when the consultants come to a different conclusion to the management. When such a difference of opinion occurs there can be problems for the consultant and under such circumstances the assignment is not likely to last very long.

Of course these five different orientations of consulting work are not necessarily mutually exclusive. You could find yourself being initially engaged in a creative or lateral thinking assignment, which then develops into a procedural piece of work, or even hands-on work.

The following is a list of 30 areas of IT consulting specialization, which are frequently offered and for which there is a strong need. This is in no way a definitive list as there are literally hundreds of niche areas in IT consulting that you might find yourself considering. It is important that you take time to make a decision and to carefully work out how you will sell yourself in your chosen area. It is also useful to consider what your fallback areas of competence will be in the event that you are not successful in your primary core competency.

4.3 Key areas of IT consulting opportunity

4.3.1 Quality assurance

Quality assurance concerns itself with the delivery of a fully functioning robust application. It attempts to iron out bugs in the systems development life cycle as early as possible on the basis that it is much more cost effective to do this than to repair problems after the software has been commissioned. It is a very demanding control area which is not always seen as being central to the actual production of the application. This type of work requires an especially detailed or picky approach and is therefore not always seen as being a popular area in which to work. Quality assurance is therefore an area in which there is a continual demand for good consulting services as there are still numerous organizations that need help in setting up effective quality assurance programmes.

4.3.2 Project management

Despite the enormous energy and investment that has been committed to project management in terms of software development and of course training, it remains a problematic area for many organizations. Projects, and especially IT projects, are notoriously over budget and behind the original planned schedule. Projects encounter problems from a wide variety of sources many of which have little if anything to do with the technology that is being employed. Extensive opportunities exist to take over projects which have lost their project manger, to teach projects managers and other members how to use software to help plan and control their work and also to understand and control their project risks. This is really a field that can offer good potential for any IT consultant with a new angle on how to improve project performance.

4.3.3 Data warehousing and mining

Although now established for some 10 years or so the field of data warehousing and mining offers considerable opportunities for consulting. Data warehousing and mining is a topic that has by no means reached its peak. The setting up of the application software for this type of work is not trivial. Furthermore there are extensive opportunities associated with helping clients interpret the results of data mining. Some of this work may be fairly statistical and thus it could suit IT consultants who wish to develop a more technical type of consultancy practice. Knowledge of software application products such as SAS and SPSS may well be helpful to individuals wanting to get into this area.

4.3.4 Market intelligence

The area of market intelligence is a very neglected field, which is of considerable importance to any effective IT department. The challenge is to be able to continually monitor major IT products and important IT suppliers. This type of work might suit you if you are an avid reader of journals, newspapers, magazines and websites. You would need to be able to present up-to-date information to your client on a regular basis. One of the many ways to approach this type of consulting is to write a regular column for a relevant industry publication, which would necessitate the collection of regular data and commenting on market changes. To make a success of this end of the IT consulting spectrum you will need to be able to take sales hype and make real practical sense of it.

4.3.5 Client–server applications

The term client–server has been a buzzword for the past 15 years or so. This approach to IT architecture has offered a considerable opportunity to enhance the efficiency and the effectiveness with which computers may be employed. Although considerable progress has been made in the use of this architecture there are still many organizations and vendors that have yet to adopt it. Consulting services are especially needed in regard to the evaluation of where and how to use this architecture and what are the appropriate strategies for optimizing its use.

4.3.6 Customer relationship management (CRM)

The field of customer relationship management is more than a little challenging for many organizations. This is due to a number of reasons not the least of which is that to effectively employ customer relationship management requires significant changes to the mind set of many if not most commercial organizations. This field has enormous potential for the IT consultant. Many organizations are still struggling with the CRM at the conceptual level. Those firms that have come to terms with what it actually means are now trying to make rational decisions about how to apply the technology. Of course some firms have gone further and those that are already down this demanding path frequently need help with training and then assistance in moving to more advanced applications of this management technology

4.3.7 Data administration

Large organizations cannot successfully use computers without there being very clear and well-enforced rules about how data is used. This includes a considerable number of different aspects of

... WELL-ENFORCED RULES ABOUT HOW DATA IS USED

systems ranging from data definitions to data access and software availability. This is not necessarily a terribly glamorous end of the IT consultancy spectrum but it is one for which there is and probably always will be a demand. Any attempt to integrate disparate applications packages without giving appropriate attention to data administration is likely to fail.

4.3.8 m-Commerce (or mobile commerce)

The rapid acceptance of e-commerce and e-business suggested that the next step in the evolutionary chain of IT developments which allows business to be conducted both remotely and also on the move, i.e. m-commerce, will become very big business too. It is of course not yet clear exactly how m-commerce will be played out. In order to make this vision a reality there are still technological challenges to be overcome. However, these should not be a major obstacle. The real action in which the IT consultant will be able to play a major role is in help to deliver revenue generating or cost reducing applications. This field is wide open and the only limitation seems to be your imagination.

4.3.9 Database applications

The original database concept in which any data set would be entered into the computer once and only once has turned out to be another holy grail or philosopher's stone. Nonetheless database technologies can make substantial improvement to the way IT departments operate. There is a very important role for skilled database applications consultants in many organizations. The issues of database distribution is a vital one as well as how to integrate disparate databases.

4.3.10 Local and wide area networks

There are a variety of different angles to this area of potential IT consulting work. There are still some firms who have not yet employed either local or wide area networks and need help with the selection and installation processes. There are those firms who need ongoing maintenance and who are not really big enough to have their own local area networks engineers and maintenance people. There is quite a lot of training issue surrounding this area, which IT consultants can help with. Another issue here is the selection of appropriate vendors and the structure of contracts. Both local and wide area networks are notoriously fragile in regard to performance and being able to advise on performance improvements is a very useful consultancy skill. There is also the question of the various housekeeping disciplines which become necessary when computers and telecommunications faculties are shared in a corporation.

4.3.11 Security

This topic will never go out of fashion. In fact there is every prospect that its importance will continue and even grow. Security problems continue to plague the IT industry. With the recent rash of viruses this area of IT management has again come under the spotlight. About once a week there are new scares of even more terrible viruses. There is also the question of hacking and of course the issues of fraud related to this. Ironically fraud has not often been given much prominence. You occasionally read about it in the newspapers or see it on television but it is generally an issue which those who have been defrauded do not want to make visible.

4.3.12 e-Government

Throughout the western world at least, and perhaps in other parts of the globe as well, government is by far the largest user of computers. Although many governments have been slow to start they are now beginning to see the value in computer applications. Both local and national government departments are increasingly adopting electronic applications. This is both in the form of standard information technology and telecommunications applications but now increasingly in the form of 'e' applications as well. The initial activity in this respect is to generate portals for the integration of the supply of information but this is being followed by e-government websites through which business can also be transacted such as tax assessing and payment sites. There is considerable demand for consultants to help provide expertise in this area.

... OFFER SERVICES IN PARTICULAR INTERNET MARKET SEGMENTS

4.3.13 Internet

The Internet encompasses such a broad spectrum of activities and services that it is difficult to be simply an Internet consultant. It is therefore important for the IT consultant to offer services in particular Internet market segments. Some examples might be quite technical such as telecommunications, mobile technology, wireless networks, while others could be more strategic, such as developing corporate Internet capabilities. There is also the question of Internet use in such basic areas as e-mail and discussion groups and conferences.

4.3.14 Intranet

More and more organizations are turning to browser-based technology as the key medium of communication and information distribution across the firm. The application list of possible Intranet opportunities is extensive. One of the problems with this area is that setting up and maintaining multiple Intranet applications is an area for which many organizations look to outside help from IT consultants.

4.3.15 Knowledge management

The potential for knowledge management to produce IT consulting opportunities is legion. Knowledge management is an area in which most business firms and other organizations know that there is much to be achieved if they can implement the right applications. However, the knowledge management field of study has innumerable concepts and no consensus of how to best go about defining and managing knowledge. In an attempt to do something many organizations have installed Intranet systems which they see as a route to knowledge management. Many of these Intranet systems are badly in need of advice from competent IT consultants.

4.3.16 Documentation

Many IT systems fail to be used properly by staff because not enough time and attention is paid to the documentation. It is often the case that the programmers and analysts involved in the development of the system are not good at providing readable end user documentation. This is often considered to be a rather boring activity, which is beyond the call of duty of a systems developer, and perhaps this may well be the case. Thus specialists are best able to produce quality software documentation. This type of work would suit you if you are good at writing and if you enjoy learning new skills. IT training can sometimes accompany documentation consulting (see below).

45

4.3.17 e-Learning

As Intranets become more accepted across organizations, so the possibility of using the computer as an interface for learning is becoming more apparent. As an e-learning consultant you might be asked to develop a training programme on processes specific to the organization, or you might be asked to implement a training programme based on an 'out-of-the-box' application.

4.3.18 Product or industry specialist

If you have launched your IT consultancy career after gaining considerable expertise in a specialist product or industry area it is a natural step to offer your skills back to the industry as a consultant. One of the advantages of this when you are getting started is that you should have a number of contacts and prospects to whom you can offer your services.

4.3.19 Website development

This is a very fashionable form of IT consulting today. This type of work can be suitable for consultants who prefer to work from home, as usually most of the development work does not need to be carried out on the client's premises. It is important to have some sample websites to show potential clients as many firms choose their developers based on either word of mouth or on work that they have seen and liked. It is important not to bite off more than you can chew with this type of work, as it is all too simple to take on assignments and then not be able to deliver on time.

4.3.20 e-Business opportunities

Although e-business is not as fashionable as it was recently it is still a vital application area for many organizations in both the business and government arenas. Within the e-business framework there are numerous applications areas, which range from setting up entirely new businesses, which are serviced by the Web to using the Web to enhance the current business processes. As this type of development frequently requires new mind sets as well as new skills there are plenty of opportunities for IT and other business consultants.

4.3.21 e-Business model development

It is one thing to set up an attractive website but it is an entirely different matter to make any money out of it. e-Business model development is about understanding the costs and revenues associated with Web enhanced businesses. Here IT consultants can play a major role in helping organizations understand the work involved in setting up a Web.

4.3.22 Helpdesk

As the number of processes run by IT increase, so there is a greater need to provide continuous help for staff. However, the operation of an IT helpdesk is an overhead that many organizations are not prepared to carry with full-time staff and thus it is a job that can be outsourced to one or a team of IT consultants. If you have expertise in a specialist area such as SAP or Oracle, then it is likely that you will be able to find work in organizations that have developed applications in these systems. There is also a need for a more generalized helpdesk supporting staff with productivity tools such as e-mail, PC packages, peripherals, etc.

4.3.23 Desktop publishing

... THOSE WHO CAN COMBINE DTP WITH WEB DEVELOPMENT SKILLS

Most organizations have to publish a wide range of material for numerous reasons. There are now many options available as to how to achieve this and to understand the issues in this field is still a complex challenge for some organizations. This is especially the case as the term publishing no longer refers to the paper medium only. With the arrival of the Web and the importance associated with efficient and effective corporate websites, desktop publishing has been given another although slightly different lease of life. There are huge opportunities for those who can combine desktop publishing with Web development skills. In fact much of the growth in Web consultancy has come from this particular arena in the past few years.

4.3.24 Vendor selection

The problem of vendor selection has become much more demanding in recent years with the arrival of a large number of quite competent vendors of hardware and software and other services. If you have come into IT consultancy from an IT sales or marketing environment, this type of work might suit you well. The work required here is often substantial with the client organization needing to prepare an invitation to tender in the first instance. Then there is often considerable work involved in short listing numerous responses to the invitation to tender before focusing on the final selection of the supplier. Knowledge of computer contracts will also be very useful in this type of work. At the heart of this end of the spectrum of IT consulting is the real ability to see through the sales hype and know what a vendor can really do for you.

4.3.25 Recruitment

Recruitment is a traditional source of work for IT consultants. Of course it is a highly specialized activity and thus requires considerable preparation before taking this on as an additional consulting activity. However, IT consultants frequently encounter requests from client firms for them to help find a suitable individual to fill a particular type of role. One of the issues which arises here is that the remuneration paid for this type of work is usually based on a different method of calculation than traditional IT consulting fees. Furthermore there is sometimes a guarantee that the new incumbent to the job will remain in post for a minimum period. If this does not happen then the recruitment fee is sometimes refundable.

4.3.26 IT training

The training requirement associated with IT is very substantial in many organizations. There is substantial training required for IT professionals as well as for large numbers of application systems users. As an IT consultant you can be involved in either the assessment of training needs, planning or scheduling of training. There are also large projects that focus on the development or the delivery of IT training, or perhaps even both. As the application software is continually changing this is an area in which a consultant's work is hardly ever finished. The delivery method of training within organizations is usually restricted by geography, time, cost and thus e-learning is an area that is becoming more popular.

4.3.27 Computer telephony integration (CTI)

There is currently major interest in the relatively new field of computer telephony integration. Computer telephony integration is the basic technology that you need to master if you intend to operate efficient and effective call centres. As call centres have become a very important issue, especially in larger business firms and other organizations, there is considerable potential here. Here in addition to obtaining help on technical matters of integration, consultancy advice is often needed for decisions involving issues such as deciding whether to outsource or perform the work in-house.

4.3.28 Business process reengineering (BPR)

Business processing reengineering, or business processing redesign as it is sometimes referred to, has been a fruitful area for IT consultants since it was first launched some 10 years ago. Although not many organizations obtained the improvements in their business performance they sought through this approach, it has nonetheless remained a popular field for IT consultants to pursue.

4.3.29 Strategic IS planning (SISP)

Strategic IS planning is an area in which there is substantial potential for IT consultants. Not many organizations have successfully resolved how to match their IT activities with their corporate planning requirements. As a result there are plenty of opportunities for IT consultants in this field.

4.3.30 Business continuity planning (BCP)

The field of BCP has developed from the set of issues related to ensuring adequate backup in the case of a catastrophic loss of your IT facilities. This field of interest used to focus on how an organization could cope if all its data were lost or stolen, or if a computer were to be destroyed as a result of a major incident, such as flood or fire.

A standard strategy was to ensure that all the organization's hardware and software was duplicated and stored in another location, some distance from the computer site. In addition arrangements were often made with vendors to have backup computers available in the event of such incidents.

BCP, due to current international tensions and uncertainties, is an expanding area for IT consultants.

	PM	MI	CRM	mC	N/W	Sec	eG	Inter	Intra	Trn
Project Management (PM)	80%									
Market Intelligence (MI)		60%								
CRM			40%							
m-Commerce (mC)				40%						
Networks (N/W)					40%					
Security (Sec)						60%				
e-Government (eG)							100%			
Internet (Inter)								80%		
Intranet (Intra)									60%	
IT Training (Trn)										70%

Figure 4.1 Consultancy Opportunity Matrix showing initial evaluation ratings

	eG	Inter	PM	Trn	Sec	Intra	MI	N/W	mC	CRM
e-Government (eG)	100%									
Internet (Inter)		80%								
Project Management (PM)			80%							
IT Training (Trn)				70%						
Security (Sec)					60%					
Intranet (Intra)						60%				
Market Intelligence (MI)							60%			
Networks (N/W)								40%		
m-Commerce (mC)									40%	
CRM										40%

Figure 4.2 Consultancy Opportunity Matrix sorted by competence rating

4.4 The Consultancy Opportunity Matrix

The following Consultancy Opportunity Matrix (COM) is a useful tool to perceptually map the consultancy opportunities available to you.

The matrix is initially constructed by putting down the areas of competence you feel you have acquired over the last five or so years.

Figure 4.1 shows a selection of 10 different consultancy opportunities. In this example the consultant considers the main area of competence as being e-government and thus has rated this 100%. Each of the other consulting areas on the list has then been evaluated in terms of his or her competencies in a similar fashion. In Figure 4.2 the matrix has been sorted by competence rating.

As has already been suggested, it is not a good idea to proclaim expertise in too many areas – even if you have such expertise,[4]

---

[4] This is simply a question of the fact that a jack-of-all-trades is so often perceived as a master of none. Of course some people are actually able to deliver in multiple areas but you need to be careful if you take this approach.

a cut-off line point needs to be established. It is probably useful to establish an 80% rating as a cut-off point. Thus anything you don't feel at least 80% confident in you would not consider selling.

This means, in the above example, that the consultant could market his or herself in the areas of e-Government, Internet Usage and Project Management.

Although it could be argued that it is not really necessary to include on your matrix areas of consulting that would rate relatively low, you might decide to draw up a matrix of all the areas you feel that you could work in and then be realistic about those that you are in a position to undertake work in now.[5] These high rated areas will then form the basis of your marketing plan.

4.5 Consultancy Opportunities by Industry Matrix

As well as considering your competence in specific areas of consulting, there is also the question of which industry sectors you feel you are competent to work in. Figure 4.3 is a Consultancy Opportunities by Industry Matrix (COIM), which looks at the same 10 areas of consulting used in the previous example in conjunction with seven different industry sectors.

The COIM matrix has been created by taking the 10 areas of competence, sorted by competence rating, used in the previous

	Banking	Education	Financial Services	Government	IT Suppliers	Manu-facturing	Pharma-ceuticals
e-Government (eG)		4	3	1	2		
Internet (Inter)	1	1	1	1	1		
Project Management (PM)	3	2	3	1			
IT Training (Trn)							
Security (Sec)							
Intranet (Intra)							
Market Intelligence (MI)							
Networks (N/W)							
m-Commerce (mC)							
CRM							

Figure 4.3 Consultancy Opportunities by Industry Matrix

[5] Effective consultants continue to learn throughout their careers and so your skills will evolve and you will become confident to expand or change your horizons. This learning often comes from doing the work for the client which some clients have been known to resent – they can sometimes unfairly say 'the only thing the consultant did here was to learn how to do the job'.

example. These are then ranked or mapped by the consultant's personal preferences to different industry sectors.

From the above matrix you can see that the consultant is really most competent in Government, but could undertake e-Government assignments that were linked to education, financial services or IT suppliers. If the work that is actually obtained is focused on the Internet, the industry sector is not so relevant to this consultant, and thus an equal ranking has been put across the industry sectors of banking, education, financial services, government and IT suppliers.

Depending on the area of consulting you are intending to work in, it might be appropriate to produce a more detailed matrix that considered sub-sections of a particular industry. For example, if you felt that you are qualified to work only in government or the public sector related areas, industry options in the matrix might be Local Government, National Government, Public Corporations, etc.

4.6 Summary and conclusion

There are so many different options within the field of IT consultancy that a chapter like this can only scratch the surface.

It is important that you be really quite honest, if possible absolutely honest, with yourself about exactly where your competencies lie. Once you have identified them then you should focus on selling these skills to your prospective clients. But don't expect instant results. It can take a bit of time before you achieve a breakthrough. Quitting too early can be a problem. However, if you are not successful within a few months you may have to expand the range of competencies that you are offering. Beware of straying too far from where your real skills are. If it becomes clear that you are taking a chance then you may well find yourself in difficulties.

4.7 Checklist

Things to think about when considering the consultancy options

1 What is your personal core competency?
2 Are you satisfied that you are highly competent and have an in-depth knowledge and are thoroughly experienced in this field?

3 What sort of assignments will you first look for:
   (a) Creative or lateral thinking assignments
   (b) Experiences-based assignments
   (c) Procedural assignments
   (d) Hands-on assignments
   (e) Responsibility assignments.
4 In what industry would you most like to work?
5 If your core competency isn't selling (and it probably won't be) how do you intend to sell the skills that you have?
6 Are you planning to add to your set of core competencies and how do you intend to do this?

Pick your service offerings

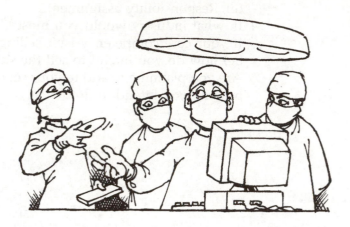

Everything that can be invented has been invented.

Charles H. Duell, Commissioner, US Office of Patents, 1899.

In the previous chapter I listed some of the more obvious avenues of IT consulting and suggested how you might focus on a particular competence or even a couple of competencies that you will offer to the market. Once you have chosen the field in which you believe you are most competent then you need to structure service offerings in that field. This means selecting an activity and pricing it – in fact sorting out all the terms and conditions.

5.1 Generally don't do the same as everybody else

You will have noticed from Chapter 4 that there are a wide range of opportunities available. I listed only 30 but in reality there are probably over a hundred. However, the real challenge that all start-up IT consultancies face is to come up with a new service or a new angle to offer the market. It is very hard to make a success of any business if you start trying to do the same as everybody else. You have just got to find some way of differentiating yourself from all the other operators out there. You have to create a compelling reason why people will buy from you and if at all possible your offering should be in some way or another unique.

Finding a unique or new angle can be very difficult indeed and it is easy to feel daunted by this task. There is no easy route to finding this new angle on the type of service you intend to offer. It is a question of relentlessly looking for opportunities and then discussing these with people who you believe will be able to give you an objective view and some good advice. It is just not possible to know in advance what will actually work. Some apparently good ideas that have been really well researched turn out to be failures and ideas that have been thought of as 'crackpot' have actually been financial winners. It is just not possible to foresee the future. To emphasize this point:

5.2 Even world famous experts get it wrong!

I list here a number of comments made by experts who either accepted traditional orthodox views which could have stood in the way of really great projects or who just rejected new ideas out of hand. Thus in 1943 Thomas Watson Sr, the then chairman of IBM, rejected the notion of the company become involved in computers. His historic comment was 'I think there is a world market for maybe five computers.' Of course it is only fair to say that at that particular time computers were involved in doing only large and tedious calculations for the military. Nonetheless visionaries like Alan Turning had already noted what computers could potentially offer as far back as the 1930s.

In a similar vein to Thomas Watson Sr, *Popular Mechanics*, the best selling American magazine for technical boffins, said in an article entitled 'Forecasting the Relentless March of Science in 1949', 'Computers in the future may weigh no more than 1.5 tons.' Of course by this stage the transistor had not been developed and computers where still running on vacuum tubes. We had to go through the transistor age before we could get to the integrated circuit.

Nearly 10 years later in 1957 the editor in charge of business books for Prentice Hall was reputed to have rather pompously announced that, 'I have travelled the length and breadth of this country [the USA of course] and talked with the best people, and I can assure you that data processing is a fad that won't last out the year.' It is hard to know who he included in his category of the 'best people'! And again just over a decade later in 1968 an engineer at the Advanced Computing Systems Division of IBM

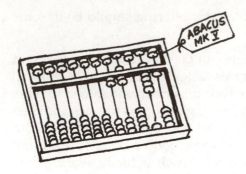

THERE IS NO REASON ANYONE WOULD WANT A
COMPUTER IN THEIR HOME

is said to have exclaimed when looking at an early microchip, 'But what . . . is it good for anyway?'

To this collection of miscalculations it is certainly necessary to add Ken Olson, president, chairman and founder of Digital Equipment Corp., who went on public record in 1977 as saying that 'there is no reason anyone would want a computer in their home'. It is difficult to understand how Olson, who played such an important role in the migration of the computed industry towards mini-computers, was so incapable of comprehending the importance of the next logical step and seeing that it would impact people's lives in a much broader way than computing had before – right into the home.

And of course this list would be woefully incomplete without the comment from the richest man in the world, Bill Gates, uttered in 1981, who will always be remembered for the insightful comment about the need for computer memory, '640K ought to be enough for anybody'.

Being flexible
A few years ago a well-known IT director from a large plc packed in his job to become an IT consultant specializing in helping IT departments develop technological visions for their organization. He was a well-known and well-liked individual who had an extensive personal network. During the first three months of his new business life he had several offers from acquaintances to help their organizations set up IT architectures and implement project management controls, etc. He refused all of these on the grounds that he was only interested in technological vision type work. Within six months these offers dried up. But he was able to attract only a trickle of technological vision type work and thus one year after he set out on his own he was in the market for a full-time permanent job.

The final quotation provided here is from Steve Jobs shortly after he and Steve Wozniak had understood what a microprocessor could actually do and before he started up the Apple Corporation. As Steve put it, 'So we went to Atari and said, "Hey, we've got this amazing thing, even built with some of your parts, and what do you think about funding us? Or we'll give it to you. We just want to do it. Pay our salary, we'll come work for you." And they said, "No." So then we went to Hewlett-Packard, and they said, "Hey, we don't need you. You haven't got through college yet." '

These stories have been provided to illustrate how easy it is to be wrong about new ideas and to help you not to become too depressed if your ideas are not at first recognized as being great.

5.3 There is no infallible way

Coming up with good business ideas is very hard indeed. If it weren't there would be far more rich people in the world.

Although there is no infallible way of producing sound business ideas there are a few steps that can be helpful in guiding you towards possible good ideas. These steps should be seen as a filter, which will hopefully pick out suggestions that are not likely to work. But do really remember there is no guarantee – great ideas have been know to fail and sometimes even the silliest ideas can actually be made to work.

The first issue that needs addressing is the novelty of the suggested service offerings. Not many of us will be able to think up totally unique schemes. There are just too many other consultants out there with active imaginations to be able to be unique. However, if you are to succeed your proposed service offerings need to be relatively novel. What this means is that you should not go into the market place and compete head on with the same offering from an already established firm.

Trying to be different and at the same time make money is not easy. Many of the Dot.Coms that went broke over the past few years seemed to me to have had only one strategy – to do things differently and they didn't seem to care at what cost. You always have to worry about the costs. If there is no profit in it then think very carefully about getting into the business. You may possibly have a loss leader for a short time but not for long as the cash resources will inevitably run out.

5.4 Differentiator versus cost leader

One useful way of thinking about the type of service offering you might pursue is to use the Porter generic strategy model. This model says that you will get clients either by offering a better quality service, this is called being a differentiator, or by proposing a less expensive price for a good service, this is called being a cost leader. If you choose a better quality service you can charge a price premium, which of course you are unable to do if you follow the other strategy. Every start-up IT consultant should think through which of these approaches he or she wants to take. Porter is not the only strategy guru with good ideas about how to direct your business and those who are interested should read the work of both Porter and Treacy.

Treacy does not offer two alternatives for your strategy but actually three. Two of these are quite similar to Porter's but Treacy also suggests that you could have a strategy of customer intimacy where you get to know your client(s) very well and you offer them a customized service. This is often quite an attractive strategy for a small start-up IT consultancy.

There are references to the thinking of both Porter and Treacy in the reading list in Appendix A.

5.5 Imagination is the key

Despite the various models there are available to help you think through your service offerings, at the end of the day by far the most important tool that you have at your disposal is your imagination. You have to be able to think as some of the American gurus would say 'outside of the box'. If you can't do this you are probably at a disadvantage. There are two quite lovely quotations from Lewis Carroll's Alice in Wonderland which I find very helpful when I need to think out of the box. The first of these quotations is from *Through the Looking Glass*:

> *'One can't believe impossible things,' said Alice.*

> *'I dare say you haven't had much practice,' said the Queen. 'When I was your age, I always did it for half-an-hour a day. Why, sometimes I've believed as many as six impossible things before breakfast.'*

Every would-be IT consultant needs to practise thinking and believing out of the box much like this.

The second quotation is *also* from *Through the Looking Glass*:

> *'I don't think they play fairly, at all fairly,' Alice began in a rather complaining tone. '. . . They don't seem to have any rules in particular. At least if there are, nobody attends to them.'*

This also encourages me to think out of the box and to come up with new imaginative ways to present service offerings when starting up a business. However, don't be too worried if not everyone to whom you present your new ideas shows great enthusiasm.

Given the fact that you have come up with an idea for novel service offerings and that you can competitively price it, then you need to work out the detail of your marketing plan and your financial forecasts, etc. Chapter 10 discusses the various financial statements, which you will need to draw up. It is important to remember that the great e-bubble of 2000 and 2001 clearly demonstrated the crucial role of profit and cash in order for your IT consultancy business to survive. In short you need to balance your imaginative and creative side with the reality of the finances.

5.6 Summary and conclusion

You need to look hard for a new angle. If you can think of going into business with only a well used service offering and no distinctive features then you may have problems. Take advice from everyone but remember that the experts can be completely wrong. So don't give up too easily even if you are not being acclaimed for your wonderful ideas.

6 Finding clients for your IT consulting business

The ideas of economists and political philosophers, both when they are right and when they are wrong, are more powerful than is commonly understood. Indeed the world is ruled by little else. Practical men, who believe themselves to be quite exempt from any intellectual influence, are usually the slaves of some defunct economist.

John Maynard Keynes, *The General Theory of Employment, Interest and Money*, 1936.

An understanding of how to find clients for your IT consulting business requires first of all an understanding of the nature of entrepreneurship.

To be a successful IT consultant means that you have to be highly capable in a number of different fields. Clearly you have to be an accomplished IT professional, but that's not enough. You also have to be a perceptive marketing manager so that you can conceive of and execute a marketing strategy for your services. In addition you have to be capable of selling, which of course

Finding clients

The single most important issue the new IT consultant has to face is finding clients. Clients are the life and soul of any business. With satisfactory clients, i.e. those who pay promptly the fees you ask, your business will prosper. Without satisfactory clients a business will certainly fail.

is a quite different skill set to marketing.[1] Once your business has begun to succeed then you will begin to employ others and you will need general management skills. Thus you need to have a plan as to how you are going to master marketing management, salesmanship, sales management, financial management and then general management. In fact quite a tall order! But in reality not necessarily as difficult as it may look.

However, even more than all these skills together, it is essential that you be an entrepreneur. Sometimes it is thought that entrepreneurship is a skill much like sales management or financial management. But it is also said that it is a fundamental personality characteristic as the essence of entrepreneurship goes far beyond simply having knowledge or acquiring skills.

6.1 Entrepreneurship – the name of the game

Being an entrepreneur is about being several things and having a number of different skills and especially attitudes at one time. Entrepreneurship is no one single thing or skill but rather a package of attributes. Entrepreneurship is about being able to spot opportunities that others do not see. It is about knowing what type of new product or service will actually be needed and for which there will be a demand.[2]

Entrepreneurship means being able to identify the type of organization that could become a client for you. It also involves an understanding of whom in your prospective corporate client you might

> **Learning to be an entrepreneur**
>
> There are a variety of courses on the subject of entrepreneurship and on setting up your own business. It is probably worth your while to attend at least one of these just to get another opinion as to what is actually involved in setting up a business and successfully running the operation. Appendix C provides you with a list of some of these courses. You will of course find many more training events and seminars if you surf the Web.

---

[1] Selling skills are often thought of as being much more prosaic than marketing and involve such issues as knowing how to listen to your prospective client and when and how to ask for the order. However, it needs always to be remembered that no matter how smart the marketing a sales contract or letter has to be obtained before the actual work can begin.

[2] It is important to note that there is a difference between need and demand and that one of the key issues that distinguishes between these two concepts is the question of price. There are all sorts of needs that do not translate into demand simply because the price is inappropriate. Thus one of the key attributes of the entrepreneur is estimating the elasticity of price demand for whatever he or she intends to do, make or sell.

approach to buy your service. This issue of finding the right person to talk to is a big challenge especially when you want to do business with large organizations where it is notoriously difficult to find the right person to approach. You may have to be quite persistent and go back to the organization several times before you find the right person.

... SKILLS ARE CERTAINLY INVOLVED IN BEING AN ENTREPRENEUR ...

Entrepreneurship also requires competence at knowing how to set up a business in such a way to take advantage of these new ideas. It also involves being sensitive to the risks involved and being able to assess these risks. Entrepreneurship also requires you to be able to manage these risks well.[3]

Thus skills are certainly involved in being an entrepreneur but entrepreneurship does normally go well beyond clearly or easily learnable skills. For example, when it comes to the central entrepreneurial issue of risk taking it is not at all certain that being able to take a risk in business is actually a teachable skill rather than a personal characteristic. No matter what their formal training some people are simply risk averse. Thus there is some debate as to whether entrepreneurs are born to this way of thinking or if entrepreneurial ability can be taught and thus actually learnt.

Whatever the case, unless you have a fair share of the abilities of an entrepreneur you might as well not try to set up your own IT consulting business. Your entrepreneurial flair is what is going to drive your business and it will be

The spider web approach
Ultimately finding clients for your IT consulting business is about building a network of clients and others who are favourably disposed towards your business efforts. Building this network can begin months before you leave your employment and if you do this you will find the start-up months much easier. This network may be built up much like a spider develops a web. The spider places anchor points at strategic places and then joins them up with a series of threads in order to make the web. It's a phased development approach as is the development of a network of potential clients.

[3] Some of the famous entrepreneurs who have been celebrated over the years have not been good at understanding and managing the risk that their businesses have faced. One famous example that comes to mind is Sir Freddie Laker who without doubt revolutionized the airline business but who apparently did not foresee the risk in rapid expansion.

your skill as an entrepreneur that will largely direct your client finding successes. Getting to know if you are sufficiently entrepreneurial before you start your IT consultancy business is a challenge. This may not become obvious until you actually start. The act of starting up on your own is a very entrepreneurial move in itself and this will discourage many armchair captains of industry. One of the ways of feeling your way into entrepreneurship is to start up your IT consultancy business only after you have secured your first assignment. There are two ways of doing this. The easiest, cleanest way is to negotiate a deal with your employer. Your employer may find it advantageous to reduce the head count but at the same time the organization may still need your skill, perhaps not full time, at least for the time being. If you are in such a situation you might be able to negotiate a one or two day a week assignment with your employer. This is an ideal way to start your own IT consultancy business.

> **Value for money**
> It is virtually impossible to define the term value for money. However, one way of looking at it or thinking about it is that a product or service would be considered value for money if the client felt that they were perfectly satisfied with it to the extent that they would purchase it again and perhaps pay even more for it than they originally did. In short, value for money exists when the client feels that there is no question about the fact that the product and/or service performed in the way that they expected it to do, given the price that they paid.

The second way is to make it known to your acquaintances and associates, but perhaps not your colleagues, that you are considering starting up on your own and that if they have a need for your services you would be pleased to see if you could help them. Even if nothing comes directly from this it is probably a useful way of conducting a type of market research. If no one shows any interest in acquiring your skill set then perhaps you should rethink your idea of starting up your IT consultancy business. Note there is a possible danger in this strategy if your employer finds out what you are doing. It could be argued that you are setting up your business on your employer's time and this could be grounds for your being dismissed. Of course if you are committed to leaving your employment you might not care too much if you have to face such a crisis. But it is probably better to avoid this type of situation. However, if you can possibly manage it, having a fee-paying client on the day you start your new business is indeed a great advantage.

6.2 Entrepreneurship is not enough

The virtual network

Small start-up IT consultancies can profit enormously from establishing as soon as possible a virtual network. A virtual network is simply a list of other consultants, normally self-employed or from other smaller firms, who are prepared to work for you if you obtain a large assignment that you cannot handle on your own or with your limited resources. I like the word virtual because the individuals concerned need seldom if ever meet. As well as providing extra hands which can work side by side with you, such a network can also be used to provide different skill sets which you do not have. Thus in your virtual network you might have marketing consultants, financial consultants and operations management consultants to mention only three function areas other than IS. Establishing a virtual network is not a trivial matter as you really need competent people who you can trust on your list and these are often not easy to find. Conceptualizing your virtual network and making it work is not easy but it can be of a tremendous help in ensuring success. However, do remember that members of your network can try to muscle in on your business. Or your clients can solicit them. So take care.

However, entrepreneurship alone is not enough. What is also needed is a systematic approach to understanding the market and to converting prospective clients into satisfied customers. In fact undisciplined entrepreneurship can be as much of a problem in starting up your IT consultancy business as not enough entrepreneurial flair or insight. There is no doubt that to succeed you are going to need a complex set of skills and attributes and many people do not possess these. If these skills and attributes were common there would be far more successful IT consultants than there are today.

By the way, with all the things that you will have to learn and all the skills and attitudes that you will have to develop it is probably true to say that if you take on the challenge of creating your own consulting business and especially an IT consulting business you are committing yourself to life-long learning and relearning – more than in most other professions. This will mean finding the time to read and to attend courses throughout your IT consulting career. Of course the IT consulting work itself will be a great learning experience but it will not on its own be enough.

6.3 From business strategy to marketing strategy

In the first chapter you saw that you needed to answer three key business strategy questions related to what service you are going to be offering, to whom you are going to be offering it and why anyone will buy from you. You now need to translate the answers to these high-level business questions into a marketing strategy.

6.4 Marketing strategy

Even as a small start-up IT consultancy business you will need to give a lot of thought to your marketing strategy which will include issues such as what you are actually selling, your fee level, your target market, how you will segment the market and how you will differentiate yourself, how many clients you would like, your promotion materials, etc.

However, as a first step your marketing strategy will have to address the following three issues:

1 How do you convey to the market exactly what it is that you can do?
2 How do you make your competence clear to your prospective clients?
3 How do you ensure that you are perceived to be offering value for money?

To make sure that these three important things happen you need to:

1 Have a clearly defined IT offering.
2 Express the value of the offering in a marketing document or brochure.
3 Ensure that your message gets into the right hands, i.e. that someone with an interest or a need and the money to spend receives it.

6.5 Have a clearly defined IT offering

Many potential IT consultants are really quite versatile with the possibility of offering a range of different services or solutions[4] to prospective clients. However, out of all the different IT consulting services that you might offer you need to focus on something quite specific. It needs to be an area in which you have considerable expertise and in which you can deliver real

[4] It is important for the IT consultant always to think in terms of solutions for their clients. Consultants are employed to solve problems or to help take advantage of opportunities and the consultant needs always to be on the lookout to be helpful in these ways. There really is no other rational reason why a consultant should be employed by any organization.

benefits for your prospective clients for a price that they will consider value for money. In general terms the more focused your offering the better.[5] Of course you may be able to deliver a number of different services and in the course of a relationship with a client you may well provide different solutions at different times, but you should not appear, at least initially, to be a jack-of-all-trades who will undertake anything if the money is right. It is clear that one of the marks of the professional is to specialize and to know his or her limits.

If, for example, you decide that you will base your IT consulting business on an offer to help companies with their strategic information systems planning or perhaps risk management or information systems project commissioning assistance then you need to define carefully where you regard the boundaries or limits of this activity to be and then largely stay within them. It is indeed most important that you do not confuse the issue by trying to be all things to all people or companies. This just won't work.

On the other hand consultancy is quintessentially opportunistic. What this means is that even if you have decided to be a 'strategic information systems planning' consultant but you receive an offer to do some IT related change management work you should be sufficiently flexible to consider this work opportunity. Of course this assumes that you are sufficiently competent in IT related change management work. The issue is that flexibility – taking an assignment you weren't looking for – is at the heart of successful IT consultancy.

You need to prepare marketing material, which explains what you will actually do for a client and how you will work on a step-by-step basis. You need to make quite sure that this material details the benefits of each of these steps as well as the benefit of the consulting exercise as a whole. In all your marketing material always bear in mind that your potential clients will be looking for the value proposition for them. This is sometimes expressed as the five-finger rule which is traditionally counted on the fingers of one of your hands and says 'what's in it for me?' If your prospective client cannot clearly see what's in it for him or her then you are not likely to get an assignment or make a sale.

---

[5] As your IT consultancy business develops you may wish to relax this tight focus and take on a wider range of assignments. Then the issue will become 'How much of a specialist do you want to be or do you want to become a generalist?' However, do remember that with a few exceptions it is harder to start an IT consultancy as a generalist rather than a specialist.

By the way, the more unusual or indeed unique your service offering the better it is for you. If you come up with a new approach to strategic IS planning or to project management the more likely it is that you will win some share of the attention of the market. Not having anything new to say and being simply a me-too service provider will generally make it more difficult for you to establish yourself in the market place. Having something new to say is simply a question of your being able to differentiate yourself and it will give you the opportunity of trying to attract the interest of the press which will in effect give you free advertising which could be helpful.[6] Of course this applies equally to any part of the media. Thus if you can obtain an interview on the radio or the television, even Internet television, it would be very helpful to getting your name around.

On the question of advertising, in general paid advertising is not likely to be of great value to your start-up IT consulting business. The services of an IT consultant are seldom purchased as the result of someone seeing an advertisement.[7] Consultancy is more usually bought as a result of personal contact and after some considerable dialogue between the vendor and the purchaser. Also advertising is expensive and many start-up IT consulting businesses simply won't have the funds to buy the advertising needed to make their presence felt in the market place.[8]

6.6 Express the value of the offering in a marketing document or brochure

Make sure that you can clearly articulate the value of what you are offering. Consultancy will normally be bought only if there is a clear value proposition and if you cannot demonstrate this you will probably not get an assignment.

[6] Like most things in life this notion of having a novel idea can be taken too far and sometimes a new service can be so new that no one will recognize the need for it. If you are going to follow the strategy of low cost regular work you will probably be better off if you are not too novel in your approach.

[7] Of course there are exceptions to this comment and after all if you advertise and obtain only one new client you may well be on the right side of the financial equation. However, I have known advertisements for consulting services not to solicit even one enquiry.

[8] The issue of engaging promotional consultants or personal publicists is similar to buying advertising. It is frequently too expensive for the small start-up IT consultancy and value delivered is unlikely to be great.

HAVING A REAL EXAMPLE OF
PREVIOUSLY DONE WORK

Care needs to be taken with the marketing material – perhaps you will produce a paper brochure to indicate quite clearly the value of what you are offering. Reducing your value proposition to money terms is very helpful. If you can show that it will cost £Xs to hire you and that you may well save the organization two, three or 10 times £Xs then the prospects of your obtaining work are good. Having a real example of where you have previously done this is very helpful and of course if you can supply a reference, well that's ideal. However, being precise in a brochure is often very difficult. Perhaps detail such as the quantification of the value proposition is often better left to a specific project proposal.

6.7 Ensure that your message gets into the right hands

... ENSURE THAT IT GETS INTO THE
RIGHT HANDS

Brochure and other marketing material are of no value unless you can ensure that you can get them into the right hands. This is not a trivial problem. Some consultancies are able to target their promotion activities quite precisely but many have quite a lot of trouble with this. Accurate targeting requires you to carefully define the type of business you think is a good prospect for you and to try to attract the attention of the most appropriate person in these organizations. Targeting is a very important part of marketing and is sometimes described as segmenting the market. It will demand a lot of your attention especially in the early days of your business.

The principle behind this thinking is that there is no use spending money trying to reach people or companies who will have no interest in your services. On the other hand sometimes it is very hard to know who might actually be interested and you may not be able to or it might not be appropriate to be too specific in your targeting. A broad brush or shotgun type approach sometimes picks up unexpected prospects and clients that you had not previously thought of. Sometimes this approach can pay dividends especially if you can arrange the costs so that if you obtain one client from the shotgun distribution of your brochures, it will have paid for itself. If you decide to take this approach you might mail out thousands or even tens of thousands of brochures. You could insert the brochure into a management magazine or into

. . . UNSOLICITED MAIL BEING
IMMEDIATELY DISCARDED . . .

the newsletter of a Chamber of Commerce.[9] This will sometimes produce some leads, some of which may eventually convert to an assignment. However, there are many who would say that it is generally a very wasteful approach to selling IT consultancy. Mailing lists are notoriously inaccurate with many of the people on these lists having moved jobs. Some lists are simply invented with job titles rather than people's names being used. Also there is a very high rate of unsolicited mail being immediately discarded without being read and sometimes without even being opened by the recipient. It is possible to obtain current e-mail addresses from the Web and if you can use an e-mail type brochure you may get through to some of the right people at relatively little cost.

There is little doubt that IT consultancy is best sold through direct personal contacts and there is no easy way of developing these contacts. Some start-up IT consultants will spend the first three months of their new business life just telephoning one prospective client after another in order to try to establish contact. Generally receptionists and secretaries will refuse to put unsolicited telephone calls through to the person to whom you really need to speak. As a result you may well find yourself compromising your objective and settling for trying to obtain some information from the target firm – at least finding out the name and job title of a suitable person to which to send a letter and a brochure. Also sometimes receptionists and secretaries can inadvertently give clues to what sort of IT consulting services the organization might actually need. These need to be listened to.[10] This is clearly very hard and very time consuming work indeed. But sometimes there is no other way of getting started.

[9] On one occasion I inserted an expensive glossy brochure offering IT consulting services into the mailing of a Chamber of Commerce. Although I did not get an immediate reply I eventually obtained an enquiry which led to a consultancy project which paid more than ten times the cost of the brochure and the Chamber of Commerce's fees. However, this was actually a very long shot and was more like to going to the casino than making a rational marketing decision.

[10] The art of selling is a very challenging one. It is sometimes thought to be about being positive and making a big impression on the prospective client. In reality the most important aspect of selling is about listening – active listening. You will not sell anything (except by accident) if you don't know what the prospective client wants. Fortunately many if not most prospective clients will tell you what they want if you ask the right questions and then carefully listen to their answers. Active listening can be difficult especially for the more extroverted sales person. So practise it – lots.

Perseverance or determination is a key feature of the successful IT consultant.

Of course the likelihood of obtaining IT consultancy business from a brochure even when accompanied by a personal letter, which has been mailed to someone whom you have not at least spoken to, is as I already mentioned a long shot.[11]

6.8 Making your competence clear to your prospect clients

Selling is always mega-important

All businesses ultimately succeed or fail according to their ability to sell. Selling is the key. However, this is perhaps more intensely the case for the IT consulting business because consulting is quite difficult to sell and this difficulty is often not realized by the start-up IT consultant. It takes a lot of effort to sell any business consultancy. Most organizations that you will regard as prospects will for one reason or another not buy from you. This means that you will hear a lot of 'No thanks' and no matter how politely it is put this is a rejection. You have to be able to take a lot of rejection and pick yourself up and go on to the next prospect.

It has been said that competence like beauty and contact lenses is in the eye of the beholder. Thus it is a major concern as to how you can portray an air of competence to your prospective clients. It is especially difficult to project an air of competence through a marketing document[12] or brochure.[13] It is not a trivial matter to give the appearance of being able to deliver a solution to a prospective client's problem. However, one of the key issues in this regard is that your marketing document needs to be error free. Even one minor typographical error has been known to be sufficient to spoil the document's impression of professional competence. Competence in the specific

[11] It used to be thought that a beautifully produced paper brochure was essential but increasingly IT consultants are using Websites and e-mailed brochures instead.

[12] Don't forget that your business card is also a marketing document and needs to be designed with that in mind.

[13] You don't actually need to spend a fortune on a multi-coloured glossy brochure. You can probably produce a perfectly professional document on your desktop publishing system. However, you may find it very useful to seek some advice from a professional brochure designer as to how to lay out this brochure for best effect. It is also very useful to know about colour combinations and type fonts. It is surprising how many expensive brochures are actually quite hard to read.

. . . AN AIR OF COMPETENCE TO YOUR PROSPECTIVE CLIENTS

task proposed might also be demonstrated by reference to previous work for an employer or some other organization you have been involved with. Of course if you use such references you need to make sure that you have cleared this, in advance, with the people concerned. Whatever you put in writing in your marketing document needs to be verifiable.

The question of a reference or references is a very important one and is a key to successful IT consulting selling. What this amounts to is making it clear that in your previous work situations you have solved identical, or at least very similar, problems and that you were considered to have delivered value. In this respect it helps a lot if you can describe your previous work by means of an interesting story. Storytelling is a very useful attribute for a consultant. However, as mentioned before you need to be quite clear that what you say is verifiable. There is a lot of cynicism around consultants. It is frequently said that *a consultant is someone who can read a book and who is prepared to travel*. You have to make it clear that you have done this type of work and that you know how to solve the problem and deliver value for money for the client. Thus if you have someone who will give you a reference to this effect you will have a considerable advantage and you will probably benefit from using this.

There is little doubt that the question of creating an air of competence is one of the most serious facing the IT consultant. There are many characteristics of a competent consultant that you should ensure that you are able to emulate. These include actively listening, empathizing, searching for a solution, etc. However, before you will get a chance to demonstrate these you may have to convince your prospective client through your marketing material and perhaps a telephone discussion. This is what makes the marketing material so very important.

Presenting your competence is of course best done through face-to-face contact and consultants will often undertake speaking engagements at conferences and seminars to meet people to whom they can directly present their competencies.[14] Having met a prospective client at a conference at which you were presenting or even attending can put you in an advantageous position.

[14] There are numerous opportunities for consultants to speak at conferences and seminars especially if they will appear without being paid a fee. Although this will provide visibility for the consultant it is important not to take on too much unpaid work as presenting at conferences is very time consuming.

6.9 What is your target market?

Choosing your target market is a key issue. It is sometimes thought that small start-up IT consultancies need to focus on other small businesses. Although it is possible to succeed with an IT consultancy business by operating in this business sector, this notion of needing to focus on like sized businesses is usually not useful. In general small businesses seldom buy much consulting services. They frequently don't really have the sort of problems that consultants can help with and perhaps more importantly small firms often just can't afford the cost of the consultancy time. However, there are clearly exceptions to this and some people have developed successful and substantial businesses from servicing small firms.

The next step up this size ladder is the medium sized business. This is usually a more fertile ground as some of these organizations do have the need for sophisticated information systems and also are sufficiently profitable to have the resources with which to pay for this service.

But start-up IT consultancies need not restrict themselves to thinking that they should only approach smaller firms. Most consulting is bought by big organizations that have big problems needing help and who have the money to pay for it. Therefore these organizations are a good target for the start-up IT consultant. The main problem you will face is finding out who in the large organization you need to talk to and once you have found this out, the issue is then how do you get access to this person. There is absolutely no doubt that getting access to the appropriate person is tough and you need to be resourceful to do this. If it is possible for you to get an introduction from a friend or former colleague or even a family member, this can be helpful.

You might also meet the right people at a variety of venues such as meetings of the Chamber of Commerce or professional societies or alumni clubs or hardware or software user groups, etc. It is probably worth joining a few of these even before you start up your IT consultancy business.

Of course as mentioned above some IT consultancy businesses are set up only after the entrepreneur has been able to land the first job. This could be regarded as a warm start to the business and is a very useful way to get going – in fact a great way to start

> **How many clients do you want?**
>
> Start-up entrepreneurs are sometimes surprised by this question. They instinctively feel that we all would want as many clients as we can get. But this is often untrue. A small number of financially sound clients who are willing to give you a steady stream of interesting work is probably ideal. However, the definition of 'a small number' can be tricky. In most cases two or three may be too few because if you lose one of them you may have a work and revenue crisis. On the other hand a start-up IT consultancy might find even six or seven clients quite a lot to handle.

up your own business. Having business from day one means that money can start rolling in at the end of the first month but perhaps even more important there is a great psychological or emotional advantage to begin a business from a running start. Working to find your first assignment is very stressful and if this takes more than a few months it may cause quite a lot of difficulty.[15]

If you are starting up your IT consultancy business cold then you have to expect the first few months to be especially tough. Finding clients is just not easy.

6.10 Finding your target clients

... EFFECTIVE AS YOU CAN BE IN FINDING BUSINESS

The process of identifying and contacting target clients is an important part of sales management and this is one of the key skills the start-up IT consultant needs to quickly acquire. The key issue here is not wasting any of your time.[16] You just have to be as efficient

[15] Some prospective IT consultants will just drop out and give up and go and find another job. They might in the meantime have wiped out much of their savings. Others will find the unsuccessful struggle to find work so stressful that it can actually make them ill. It is really a sad state of affairs if your prospective IT consultancy business fails and you were to end up both broke and ill. This does unfortunately happen to some people but fortunately not too many.

[16] It is of course very difficult to know in advance what constitutes a waste of time when prospecting for new business. I have been surprised several times by business coming my way when I was sure that the business lead had long since died. In general I would say that if you get work from 1 in 10 prospective clients within 90 days of making contact you are probably working relatively efficiently. Other consultants would regard this as too slow. Of course the size of the assignment also needs to be brought into this equation. You might decide to hang in much longer and try much harder if there is a really big assignment in the offering.

and effective as you can be in finding business. You need to keep track of whom you have contacted. You need to record the type of discussion you have had with people and what sort of proposal, verbal or written, you have made. A simple database on a personal computer will be a great help with this. Some sales managers make a distinction between clients, prospects and suspects. A client is someone with whom you are currently doing business. A prospect, which of course is short for prospective client, is someone you believe is likely to do business with you and a suspect is a person or an organization about which you know very little but about which you feel there may be some chance of your doing business. Using this terminology many organizations will be suspects for you and the first task you have, as your own sales person, is to establish if there is any potential business there. It's very much like panning for gold. You have to shake out the duds and then focus on what is left. And of course only part of what you are left with after the initial shake out will actually be useful to you.

In the case of the start-up IT consultancy there are at least two key questions which have to be immediately answered to decide if you actually have a suspect that will become a prospect. The first is 'Is the suspect a regular user of consultants?' and the second is 'Do they have a problem with which I can help them?' If the answer to both of these is *yes* then there is a third qualifying question, which is 'Do they have the money to pay for IT consultancy?' With three yes answers the suspect could be considered to be eligible for promotion to the status of prospect. With one or more *no* answers the suspect should be put on the back burner for possible attention at a future date.

Start-up IT consultancies will probably have lots of prospects and one of the major initial tasks is to try to prioritize them. This is sometimes difficult and always be prepared to be surprised as to who ends up giving you business and who doesn't. You need to assess the prospects in terms of the probability that they will give you an assignment. Some people try to make an objective assessment of this probability but in reality any probability assessment of this nature is essentially a subjective opinion. The prospects that you deem to have the highest probability of offering an assignment need to be wooed most carefully. The lower probability prospects must not be entirely ignored but less attention needs to be given to them.

These probabilities are not fixed. In fact they will change all the time and you will find yourself changing your mind as to who will produce your next job. To give yourself any chance of controlling this you need to fully document all the contacts that you have with your prospects. Some sales managers believe that if a prospect does not develop into an assignment within a given period of time such as three months you as your own sales person should drop that prospect off your list. It is true to say that prospects should not stay on the list forever but the period of time which you give yourself to close a deal is very subjective and probably really depends upon which other organization you have on your prospect list. Your opportunity cost needs to be kept in mind continually.

Sales management is as much an art as a science and you will find that your own success or failure will teach you a lot as you proceed in building your IT consultancy business. In general it is important to ensure that your selling efforts are highly focused and as said before you use your selling time as efficiently and as effectively as you can. Well or productively used selling time is one of the fundamental contributors to business success.

It is worth stressing again that you need to be clear as to what you want to sell and who are likely to buy from you. You need to avoid trying to sell assignments that you cannot confidently do. You need to avoid trying to sell jobs that are too big or too small. You need to avoid selling jobs, which are in locations, that are too inaccessible and thus require too much travelling time. It is important to refuse jobs that you are not comfortable that you can competently perform. It is much better to refuse an assignment than to take on something you are not really able to deliver and face a subsequent row or even a law suit with a client. In summary the single most important issue the new IT consultant has to face is finding clients. Clients are the life and soul of any business. With satisfactory clients, i.e. those who pay promptly the fees you ask, your business will prosper. Without satisfactory clients a business will certainly fail.

6.11 The project proposal

A project proposal serves several quite different functions. In the first place it is a selling document while at the same time it often serves as the basic agreement on which a contract of work may be drawn up.

There is no doubt that the project proposal is the key selling document for the IT consultant. It spells out precisely in as

Proposal expense

Some proposals are very long while others can be as short as a few pages. Big expensive consultancies sometimes spend thousands of pounds printing a proposal. This will not be necessary for the start-up IT consultant. It is entirely dependent on the assignments you are bidding for but frequently a few pages will be enough. Remember, a long rambling proposal may not be read. However, it is important to be fairly thorough and a professional presentation of your proposal documents is often quite important, especially if you are in competition with another consultant for the assignment.

Winning proposals

Winning proposals have to make the prospective client believe that you are professional, highly interested in the assignment and care about the prospective purchaser's ability to solve the problem and help him or her get the kudos for this work. The proposal needs to point out that you and the prospective client have the necessary shared objective and maybe even shared values to make the project work.

compelling terms as possible why the consultant should be engaged and what benefits the client will obtain by the end of the assignment. This document requires considerable attention to both the high level aspects of the proposed work and in some cases even to the detail of precisely what will actually be done. Sometimes a proposal can take weeks or even months to write, although months would be unusual and only happen in the case of the largest jobs. However, even for quite small jobs it is most important not to rush your proposal. Make sure that it covers all the issues you need to.

The proposal needs to be a document which explains just about everything concerning your possible involvement with the proposed assignment without you being there to explain what you actually mean. The things which are left out of a proposal often come back to haunt you and the project. Thus preparing this document is going to take time, effort and even money – and it is necessary to write the proposal well.

Therefore start out by asking your prospective client if you may submit a proposal. Do not prepare this document before you have got this go-ahead, as you don't want to waste the time on a proposal if the prospect is not going to read it and take it seriously.

Always remember that a project proposal is the IT consultant's ultimate selling document. A professionally prepared project proposal spells out what the problem or opportunity the consultant can help with actually is. The project proposal demonstrates how the consultant will help. It will itemize the deliverables. And it states clearly why and how the consultant is qualified to do this. It will detail the work to be done. It will specify how much and when the consultant will be paid.

Project proposals can be quite long, sometimes dozens of pages. Occasionally you may want to produce an even longer document up to hundreds of pages, for example. However, for the start-up IT consultant this would usually be an overkill. If you need to write a long proposal make sure that you keep the executive summary or overview short – perhaps only one or two pages and put as much of the detail as possible into appendices.

As well as producing a printed proposal you may also be asked to verbally present your ideas to key members of the client company.[17] In effect this amounts to speaking to the key members of the prospect's staff in order to impress them with the fact that you are competent and that you can produce the 'goods'. Always make sure that you do not speak for too long. Usually 10 to 15 minutes will be entirely adequate for this purpose.

If you are not a competent public speaker then you may need to be coached in this before you appear before your prospective client. It is important not to skip on preparation for such a presentation.

6.12 Clinching the deal with a contract

Some prospective clients will ask the IT consultants to sign a formal contract, especially for larger jobs. Other prospective clients will not bother with this formality and start you working with a verbal agreement or a letter or an e-mail.

Some prospective clients will be very formal and will insist on separate confidentiality contracts. Some prospective clients will require retaining the intellectual or copyright of anything which results from the work that you will do for them. There may also be clauses in these contracts with respect to restraint of trade, i.e.

---

[17] If you are not asked to speak to the management team then volunteer. The more exposure you can get to as many of the senior members of the company the better. If you are going to present to the management team make sure you are very well prepared. If you have to, learn your talk off by heart. Use as much technology as is appropriate but do not exclusively rely on it. Thus if you are going to use slides on your computer and a data projector, also bring with you overhead transparencies. Risk management is the name of this game.

trying to prevent you from working for a competitor in the future. You may need to steer your way carefully through these sometimes delicate issues. If you do not feel comfortable about a proposed contract or if you think that you may not fully understand all the ramifications of it you may well want to take advice from your lawyer.

As a minimum you should have possession of a letter or an e-mail of appointment to the assignment.

The contract or letter of appointment should indicate at the very least the following:

1 When the assignment will start.
2 Who will be involved in the work.
3 What equipment will be involved.
4 A list of specific deliverables.[18]
5 When the deliverables are required.
6 Who will decide if the deliverables are adequate.
7 How much will be paid.
8 How and when the payments of fees will be made.
9 How the parties to the contract could get out of the deal if they wish.

It is very important not to sign the contract before you have read it carefully. As a general rule you should give yourself some time to think about the details as it can be very embarrassing if something important has been left out and you want to go back to the client and ask for a contract revision. Sometimes the client will simply refuse point blank to revise the contract.

6.13 What the Internet can do for you

There are numerous ways in which the Internet can be used to help you find clients. In fact marketing on the Web has become a recognized field of study and a field of consulting in its own right and there are now several books and courses on this subject.

Once you have acquired one or more clients it is important to reflect your new-found experience on your website. Publishing testimonials and references from satisfied customers will help

[18] Stating the deliverable and when they will be achieved in the form of a table is a very useful approach. Such a table can subsequently be converted into a work schedule which could be the basis for a bar chart or network diagram for your own project management purposes.

reinforce your qualifications. If you present your competencies and examples of where you have applied them in an attractive and easy to follow manner on your website you can direct prospects to your site to learn more about what you do.

If you have written articles that may have been published on other websites include a link to them on your own site. If you have the permission you could also create on your own website an information centre about the area of your own competencies by publishing other material including interesting articles written by others. Your website could become a fulcrum for your marketing efforts.

If you have the time, consider writing something new for the site each month and send an e-mail to your clients and contacts to tell them about it. This will encourage people to return to your site and thus see the type of work you are currently doing. Keeping up the visibility is always important, and your website is a useful vehicle for this.

Search engines like websites that have external links to them. This means that if you can get your clients, suppliers, colleagues to include a link to your website on their site you are likely to be higher up the search rankings. The more specific you're offering is the better this can work for you.

6.14 Getting started

It is never too soon to start finding clients. Start putting feelers out the moment the idea of starting your own IT consultancy enters your head. Start keeping notes of whom you have met and what service they may be looking for. Put this on your computer so that you can eventually code it, file it and retrieve it in some useful way. Test your business ideas with everyone you can and listen to what they have to say. Not everyone will be positive so you don't have to be depressed if some people don't like your ideas. But listen to them and try to see what you can learn from them. On the other hand just because someone agrees with you or flatters your ideas they are not necessarily right. Beware of being flattered. The IT consultancy world is really quite tough to succeed in.

6.15 Summary and conclusion

It is very important not to underestimate how difficult it is to find clients. It is an endless job that nearly always has to be a priority. Despite what has been said during the e-business mania you just don't have a business unless you have clients.

You need to start building your network as soon as possible and to keep extending it right throughout the life of your business. Perhaps you can just never know too many people?

6.16 Checklist

Things to think about when working on finding clients

1 How clear is your market offering? Is it relatively unique? If not why should anyone buy from you? But of course beware of being too novel.

2 How can you clearly demonstrate your own competence? How can this competence be made obvious in your marketing material or brochure?

3 How can you 'prove' that you will be value for money? Have you got all the references you may need arranged in advance?

4 Can you get free media exposure – press, radio, television?

5 Have you started building your own virtual network? You can never start too soon.

6 Have you joined the right Chambers of Commerce and clubs?

7 Have you offered to give a lecture to or conduct a seminar for an appropriate user group?

8 How good is your telephone technique for getting to talk to the right person or at least getting information about who the right person is?

9 Have you designed a really eye-catching marketing document, business card and brochure?

10 Have you a strategy for getting the marketing document or brochure into the hands of the right prospects?

11 Can you write an effective or compelling proposal?

12 Can you speak well in public to a senior audience in order to sell your ideas and to sell yourself as the person who is needed to make the ideas a reality?

13 How skilled a salesperson are you? Are you good at asking the right questions? Are you a good active listener? Are you good at asking for the assignment?

14 Are you able to understand and interpret a contract?

15 Do you have a business lawyer available to help you if necessary?

Planning the IT consultancy assignment

What I tell you three times is true.

Lewis Carroll, *The Hunting of the Snark*, first published in 1876,
Macmillan, New York 1891.

There are always at least three sides to a consultancy assignment. There is the selling the assignment; there is the actual doing of the work; and then there is the getting paid. This chapter is about preparing for doing the work, which is actually a very demanding and critical part of any assignment.

7.1 IT consultant as a welcome friend

Overdoing the planning

When you read this chapter it is important that you take into account the appropriate level of planning which you need for your own particular assignments. No one will ever give you any credit for being overplanned. Overplanned means having flow charts and bar charts showing every detail of the work broken down perhaps by the hour for weeks ahead. In fact being too well planned is sometimes seen as a sign of not getting on with the real work – perhaps the consultant is putting off the start of the job.

Before you can plan the assignment you will need to get to know the organization a little as the way you will work will depend on how much help you will get from members of staff. The amount of this help will vary substantially depending on the environment in the organization. The environments in which the IT consultant will work can differ enormously. Sometimes the client organization can be very welcoming and very hospitable with the proverbial red carpet rolled out for the person who is coming to help sort out some problem. The staff often know when things are not going well and they are also often aware that for just some reason they can't sort it out for themselves. They need an outsider to help and here the outsider is perceived as a welcomed friend.

7.2 IT consultant as a threat

On the other hand IT consultants can find themselves in quite the opposite circumstances with their presence being resented as it is seen as threatening to the members of staff of the organization. In such a case the IT consultant can be treated with hostility. Consultancy assignments work best when the organization's staff is highly cooperative. They can easily fail if the staff is antagonistic. In fact, every IT consulting assignment represents the organization outsourcing part of its work. In most cases this work will usually be outsourced only if the organization is incapable of doing the work itself. This will often occur if there is a shortage of skills in the organization or if the current staff complement is so stretched that they just can't find the time to do the work themselves. Thus as an IT consultant you may well be plugging a gap for the organization. Sometimes the staff can see this as the management refusing to expand or promote people internally or just manipulating head count rules and this can be unpopular. It is simply the case that consultants are not always welcome by the regular workers. In such a situation you may have to be especially diplomatic in the way you plan and conduct the work.

7.3 Cooperation with staff is vital

... THE EXTENT TO WHICH THE CONSULTANT CAN SOLICIT THE COOPERATION OF THESE MEMBERS OF STAFF

Even where they are welcome the IT consultant will frequently have to work with a range of different people from the organization and one of the critical success factors for the assignment is the extent to which the consultant can solicit the cooperation of these members of staff. Thus one of the issues to establish during the assignment planning is who are the key members of staff with which you will be working and what is their attitude to this consultancy assignment. This identification of the assignment stakeholders[1] is a fundamental step which is often ignored and which can produce complications later in the project. One of the problems that arises is that if all the stakeholders are not supportive[2] of the project then the consultant may find that he or she does not have appropriate access to these people or to others who directly report to them. Consultancy projects cannot succeed without access.

Of course the doing of the work is a direct function of what exactly has been sold to the client and as you will have seen in Chapter 4 there are many different levels and different types of IT consultancy that you could sell. With this array of possible IT consultancy projects it is not easy to provide detailed generic advice on the subject of project planning. Each IT consultancy assignment situation is quite different and thus each and every consultancy project has to be planned and managed differently. Nonetheless there are a few general pointers that may be given in order to make the process of completing the project a little bit easier.

A signed contract or letter of appointment signals the start of the real work. But before you dive into the deep end it is really worth your time pausing to reflect on what you have to do and to plan the work in some detail. It is clear that one of the reasons that IT consulting assignments can get into trouble is due to the lack of reflection on what is actually involved or required to achieve the objectives before rushing into the work.

7.4 Covert objectives

Sometimes there are covert objectives or agendas within an assignment and if this is the case the planning phase of the project is a suitable time to discuss such issues. Some covert objectives are trivial such as requiring the IT consultant to give advice on career development to the project sponsors or client manager, in addition to the objectives stated in the proposal. On

---

[1] Ideally IT projects should have stakeholders but in reality it is often difficult to engender adequate commitment from the individuals who should be the stakeholders. Therefore some would say that participants may well be a better word to describe what actually happens.

[2] Not only will some of the stakeholders not be supportive but sometimes they can be down right antagonistic to the project. Where this happens the IT consultancy project may well be in danger of failing. The main recourse it to go to the bosses of the individuals concern and see if that helps them become more cooperative. However, consultants are often particularly vulnerable to company politics which can simply scuttle a consultancy assignment.

THIS CAN BE EMBARRASSING TO
YOU AS A CONSULTANT . . .

other occasions a covert objective could be to help a client manager find another job. This can be embarrassing to you as a consultant as you will not want to be associated with your client losing a member of staff. But it is usually not that difficult to get around this type of problem. Just give a fairly objective opinion about the job market. However, sometimes the covert agenda can be quite tricky. The consultant can be employed with the idea that he or she will end up covertly or perhaps even explicitly recommending that a member of the client staff be dismissed or perhaps a whole department should be closed down. When this happens the consultant is placed in a difficult position and there may not be an easy way out.

Attitudes towards consultants

Sometimes consultants can be seen by members of staff of the client organization as an admission of failure. This is because they feel that if they were doing the job well there would be no need for outsiders to be involved in their firm. Fortunately this attitude is less prevalent than it used to be. Nonetheless the IT consultant needs to be aware that not everyone in the organization will welcome his or her presence. Sometimes a friendly and helpful attitude on the part of the consultant can go a long way to alleviating this but other times this will make no difference.

Of course even when the project objectives are not covert difficult situations can arise. IT consultancy assignments are often seen as being the precursor to change and as you know change is not always welcome in organizations. This is especially true when change is being led or spearheaded by an 'outside' consultant. It is therefore essential that the sponsors carefully explain the objectives of the assignments to all the stakeholders. The IT consultant may well have to concentrate on being accepted by the other staff. High on the list of skills here will be communication, team building and even motivation. This can be very demanding or even tricky work indeed. It can also be very time consuming and it is important that these confidence-building activities are properly estimated and costed in the proposal. However, this emphasis on people management will not be the case for all IT consultancy assignments as some projects can be largely technical or even routine.

It is important to remember that every IT consultancy assignment is a project with a set of specific objectives, a starting point and an ending point and as such it will follow the standard project life cycle. The main objective then is to manage your consultancy work during the whole course of the project life cycle. In simple terms this means following the well-established formula for this type of project work which is to plan, organize, motivate and to continuously control.

7.5 Project planning

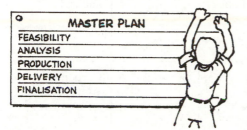

THERE IS A STANDARD APPROACH TO PLANNING . . .

There is a standard approach to planning a project and this involves identifying all the individual activities involved to achieve the objectives, then developing a work break-down and creating a work plan. In the case of IT systems development projects, identifying the stages or phases of a project can support this. Thus there will be a feasibility stage, an analysis and specification stage, a production stage, a delivery stage and a finalization stage.

It is of critical importance that you have a clear vision of what you have to do in each of these stages. As already mentioned it is indeed tempting to start the work immediately, but experience has shown again and again that if you jump into the work of the project before doing the planning correctly you will probably get the job muddled and you may end up without a satisfied client or having to do the work twice or even three times. In the context of an IT consultancy assignment most of the work of the feasibility stage should have been done at the time that the proposal was being drawn up. In a number of senses the proposal can be seen as a very high-level master plan, which includes the feasibility study. In addition to feasibility details, i.e. cost and benefits, etc., the proposal will also include critical items such as a precise list of deliverables and a timetable of when the work will be finished. All of this is needed to produce a detailed plan for the project.

7.6 A work breakdown schedule

Thus the first step in any IT consultancy project is to revisit the proposal with a view to extracting a detailed list of the actual deliverables required and the date by which they have to be completed. The next step in the planning process is to specify what are the precise activities or work elements that need to be completed in order to produce these deliverables. This is sometimes referred to as creating the work breakdown schedule or it is even called chunking the project. It is also important at

Work element	Deliverable	Duration	Person responsible
Review last five years' strategies	Summary of recurrent key issues	Three weeks	Self
Evaluation of corporate performance on key strategic issues	Matrix of key strategic issues ranked in order of perceived performance	One week	Project sponsor and self
Collection of published material from competitors relating to statements of their IT strategy	Matrix of matching competitors and strategies	Six weeks	Corporate scanning office

Figure 7.1
Typical work breakdown schedule

this stage to specify the length or duration of each activity and also who is the person responsible for the achieving of the result. This work breakdown schedule is shown in Figure 7.1.

7.7 A project management network chart

When this is completed the next task on your agenda is to determine if any of these activities are dependent on other activities. The key question here is what activities or work elements can't begin before other work elements are complete? To help answer this question you need to examine the resources required by each activity. At this stage you can then associate with each of these work parcels the type and amount of resources that you will need to achieve your activity objectives. As you can see these steps actually constitute the building blocks required to set up any project management network chart. Once this has been done then the critical path through the network of activities may be calculated.

An example of a project management network chart is provided in Figure 7.2.

The project management network chart is the first step in preparing a PERT diagram which would involve multiple estimates of times, normally the maximum, minimum and most likely periods, required to complete each activity in the network. This provides considerably more information about the manage-

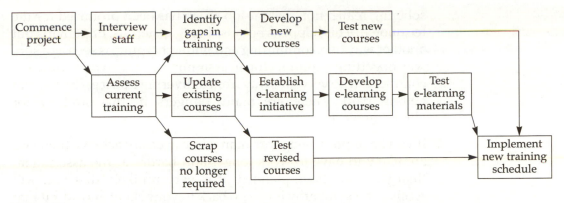

Figure 7.2
A typical project network diagram for an IT consulting assignment

ment requirements of the project. Where complex projects are being undertaken it is possible to sophisticate this diagram considerably with the use of minimum and maximum and most likely estimates for costs and other resources as well as durations mentioned above.

For a relatively small IT consultancy project this work can be done by hand in a few hours but for larger projects there are software packages available. The offerings on the market for project management are considerable ranging from simple PC-based systems costing only a few pounds to very complex midrange computer systems costing tens if not hundreds of thousands of pounds. The main advantage to a small start-up IT consultant in using a project management software package, even quite a simple one, is that once the project details have been entered on the computer it is usually easy to change the estimates and parameters of the project. Having a suitable project management software package will allow you to easily do what-if analysis on the timetable and see the real impact of proposed delays and changes.

Preparing a project management network chart for an IT assignment has often led to some surprises. When the project management network chart is completed some IT consultancy projects reveal the

Producing plans

Projects nearly always turn out to be more complicated than they first appear. There is simply a high degree of unpredictability in this type of work. The history of projects is littered with overrun on both time and budgets. It is for that reason that it is very useful to use tables, bar charts and network diagrams to describe what it is you need to do and how you will actually do it. The precise type of table or diagram you choose to use is entirely up to you but you will be much better off with some of these than with none of them.

sobering realization that far too much has been promised for the fee quoted. This happens because being generous, or perhaps put another way overcommitting and undercharging, is seen as a sure way of getting a contract for an assignment. However, getting the contract can be very far away from delivering a successful job and getting paid. There are many dangers in this strategy for obtaining work.

If you have promised more than you can easily achieve then you are likely to have to work longer and harder at the assignment than you may have planned. It is very unlikely that you will receive any sympathy if you go back to your client and admit that you hadn't quoted correctly. This is almost certainly true at the outset of the project. Perhaps as the project proceeds and you establish a good relationship and good reputation with your client, you may be able to argue that the project has actually expanded and that you now need more time or more money for your efforts.

On the other hand you may just have to consider the undercosted and thus underquoted job as a loss leader and be prepared to feel compensated for any shortfall in profit by being able to bid for and hopefully win new IT consultancy assignment from that client and others.

7.8 Bar chart diagram

Besides producing the project network diagram you might also want to produce a bar chart showing how the work is distributed during the project. This chart is sometimes produced instead of a project network diagram as it performs more or less the same function. An example of this bar chart diagram is shown in Figure 7.3. This is useful as it clearly shows[3] when

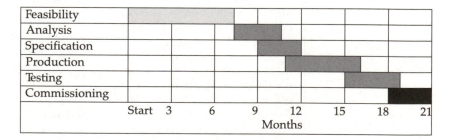

Figure 7.3
A typical bar chart for an IT project

___

[3] Bar charts often use colour very effectively to show different activities and the critical path (the critical path is defined as that series of activities or work elements in which there is no slack, i.e. if any element of this series of activities is delayed the whole project is delayed) is often shown in red.

	Today–3 months	3–6 months	6–12 months	9–12 months	12–15 months	15–18 months	18–21 months
Milestones	Project gets underway	Pilot launch of site	Launch site	First review	Second review	Third review	Fourth review
Action	Agree initial objectives.	Test team in place. Ensure site is meeting objectives.	Publicize site and work to maximize hit rate.	Corrections and minor amendments – minimal style changes.	First opportunity for significant changes and additions. Some style changes.	Revise content – minimal style changes.	Second opportunity to make significant changes and add new features.
Objectives	Establish a business plan based on objectives.	*Work within first business plan*		Prepare to amend business plan.	Amend and agree revised business plan. *Work within revised business plan*		Prepare to amend business plan.
Stakeholder involvement	Project sponsors, champion, technical team, users, etc. . . .	Essentially the technical team and pilot site users.	Marketing and technical teams.	Marketing, technical and financial teams.	Marketing, technical and financial teams.	Marketing and technical teams.	Marketing, technical and financial teams.

Figure 7.4

A typical project work breakdown chart for an IT consulting assignment various activities will overlap and appropriate arrangements can be made for these busier periods in the project. There are a large variety of other project management tools available to graphically represent or display the project plans and consultants will quickly decide which of these they personally find the most useful. Two more will be shown here.

7.9 Project work breakdown chart

IT consultants working as their own project managers will sometimes like to have a project work breakdown chart such as the one shown in Figure 7.4. This diagram has the advantage of clearly showing the timeline as well as the milestones (which are defined as especially important work elements or groups of work elements), actions, objectives and stakeholder involvement. It is a very useful document to portray a significant assignment that is conducted over a long timeframe. A particularly useful aspect of this table is the fact that milestones and stakeholder involvement are shown. Milestones represent key stages in the project and these are often delineated by special deliverables. It is important to ensure that if the project is to be delivered in stages that as many of the stakeholders as possible participate in approving the deliverable.

7.10 Making sure resources are available

Having produced either a project network diagram or a project work breakdown chart, which outlines the activities required, the next step is to ensure that all the necessary resources required to achieve these objectives are available. If you are a start-up IT consultancy business then you may be the only member of your team. But it is unlikely that you will be the only human resource – as mentioned above you will probably be working in collaboration with others from within your client organization or maybe other suppliers to the client firm. If this is the case then they need to be approached in order to ensure their understanding of their role in the IT consultancy project and to confirm their availability and then schedule them into your plans.[4] All this work is then compiled into a detailed work specification document.

[4] It is usually not a good idea to approach members of your client organization from whom you need assistance before you are correctly introduced to them. The project sponsor needs to make sure that this happens in the correct way. If the organization's protocols are not followed you may well find that the individuals with whom you need to work on the project will just not be available. Don't take any chances with this. Make sure that the right channels are followed so that all the right people are bought into the project.

Milestones	Deliverable	Activities	Resources required	Resource input	Resource availability	Target dates
Final closure of contract	Detailed IT strategic plan	Reproduce report	Self	2 months	Confirmed	31-Jan to 30-Mar
Assemble inputs to final report	Detailed IT architecture (ITA)	Summarize with ITA manager	Self and ITA officer	1 month	To be confirmed	30-Nov to 30-Dec
	Detailed hardware plan		Self and IT manager Self and software	etc.	Confirmed	01-Dec to
	Detailed software plan		Development manager		Not available – find alternative	02-Dec to
	Detailed telecommunications plan		Self and ITA manager		To be confirmed	03-Dec to
	Detailed staffing plan		Self and HR director		To be confirmed	04-Dec to
Assemble data for the ITA	Detailed systems audit	Survey hardware and software	Self and auditors		To be confirmed	21-Sep to
	Review of SWOT for each system	Collect data	Self		Confirmed	22-Sep to
	Blueprint for hardware requirements	Brainstorm with IT team	Self and IT director		Confirmed	23-Sep to
	Blueprint for software requirements	Brainstorm with IT team	Self and IT director		Confirmed	24-Sep to
	Blueprint for data requirements	Brainstorm with IT team	Self and IT director		Confirmed	25-Sep to
	Blueprint for Telecommunications requirements	Brainstorm with IT team	Self and IT director		Confirmed	26-Sep to

Figure 7.5
A detailed work specification showing deliverables, activities, individuals and dates

For anything other than a very small project this can take some time and require some effort. Figure 7.5 shows a more sophisticated work breakdown document, which contains three columns for details of resources. It also contains a column for details of the estimated start date and the finish date of the project.

If you are beginning a large assignment you may have to put several days aside for the planning while if the project is a small one then you might be able to produce the plan in a few hours.

With a completed plan the work required to organize for the project should become fairly clear. In many cases, for the IT consultant, getting organized is mostly about his or her time management. There are numerous frameworks and methods for managing your time effectively and it is important that you are familiar with at least one of these.

The question of motivation then becomes a key consideration and in this respect the IT consultant needs to ensure that he or she is not only self-motivated, but also able to offer leadership to the other project stakeholders. To be confident of being able to do this the IT consultant has to build up a trust relationship with these individuals. The extent to which this is necessary is clearly a function of the specific assignment that has been undertaken. In practice motivation can in some cases be critical to the project's success and in other circumstances it is a more minor consideration.

Finally with regards to controlling the project, meeting your project targets is crucial and you need to be able to obtain regular feedback so that you can ensure success. Control is about knowing how the project is proceeding, ascertaining if it is deviating from the plan and taking appropriate action.

Whatever the project the consultant will be partnering with the firm and its staff and perhaps its suppliers to achieve a set of objectives. Partnering really means sharing and thus there is a continuing and compelling need for the IT consultant and all the stakeholders to be as open as possible so that every one knows where they are and what is happening.

When difficulties arise it is important that they be highlighted immediately and that solutions be found before they become crises.

7.11 Project risk assessment

As a final step in planning the assignment it is useful to conduct a project risk assessment. The essence of risk assessment is to be able to anticipate the various things that can go wrong with a project before they actually happen and thus before they become a problem. Once the problem issues have been identified it is clearly easier to make plans to either avoid the problems or to minimize the impact of them if they eventually occur.

This is quite a vast subject in its own right and only a very high-level approach to this subject is discussed here. For a small project a risk assessment could be conducted in as little as one hour – for a larger project it could be a several day subproject in its own right.

The objective of a project risk assessment is to try to determine what can go wrong with the project and thus cause it to fail. Clearly the list of things that can go wrong will vary by project but there are some generic issues that should always be considered.

These risk issues fall into three groups:

1 The client
2 The work
3 The deliverables

7.11.1 The client

One of the realities of consulting is that clients can change their minds – even after a contract has been signed. Sometimes this is advantageous as it means extra work. In such a case the IT consultant will add the new aspect of the work to the contract and quote an additional fee. But sometimes it can mean that the project is reduced or even cancelled. Thus ask yourself if you think that the assignment sponsor is really committed to the project. Is the assignment sponsor's boss also committed and what about his or her colleagues? Then try to make an assessment if the assignment sponsor is committed to the organization and what will happen if he or she leaves to find a better job in the middle of the project. When an assignment sponsor leaves the project can easily be shelved. Find out if the organization is in discussions with anyone about a merger or acquisition, as this can also cause the project to be abandoned. Also ask yourself if the client can go broke and what would happen if you lose a sizable portion of your fees. As well as doing the work you really do need to be paid.[5] It is sometimes hard to say no to an assignment. But if there is a material chance that the job will blow up in your face or that you will not be paid, it is imperative that you do not take the assignment. Just do something else.

7.11.2 The work

The next step in the risk analysis is to ask yourself if you really want to do the work and if you can really do the work. Is the work doable? Is the assignment going to make the client better off? If not what will the client do when this becomes obvious? Are there any hidden work problems that may raise their heads and wreck the project? Is the project too big for you? Is the client too far away? Will you get bored with the work? Are you relying on others to do a major part of the job and what is the chance that they might let you down?

7.11.3 The deliverables

On the question of deliverables, are these too ambitious? Are there too many of them? Is the specified standard of the deliverables too low or too high? Are the deliverables sufficiently well defined? Are the various timeframes reasonable? Can you deliver without going broke? Does the client really know or understand what these deliverables are?

The final question is to ask yourself if for any reason you wish to discontinue the project do you have an acceptable escape clause? Some contracts allow for both parties to terminate the contract within a given period of notice. Other contracts may ask for a large penalty payment. It is worth knowing this in advance.

Think through each of these questions and reassure yourself that your project is relatively low risk or if it is not that you can actively do something to help reduce the risk. Don't just stand there and watch the risks turn into problems.

---

[5] There is absolutely no doubt that these are all very difficult questions and issues and that it will be no easy matter to obtain answers to these questions. However, even if you cannot find answers it is worth being aware of the sort of things that can go wrong and result in a terminated project.

7.12 Summary and conclusion

It is not easy to succeed with an IT consultancy assignment. There are numerous things that can go wrong. To help minimize problems it is really worthwhile spending some time planning an IT consultancy assignment. There are often many issues involved and to ensure you have the best chance of success put time aside to work out what challenges you face and how you will master them. Such time spent is a very sound investment and can really improve your chances of success.

Always remember that it is the client who will decide if the project was a success or a failure.

7.13 Checklist

Things to think about when planning the IT consultancy assignment

1 Create a detailed list of the required deliverables.
2 Put a delivery date against each one.
3 Break the work down into sets of logical activities.
4 Put a time estimate next to each one of these.
5 List exactly what resources are required for each task.
6 Create a work breakdown schedule.
7 Create a project network diagram for the assignment.
8 Perform risk project analysis by trying to foresee what things could go wrong.
9 Make contingency plans for those issues that could cause you trouble.
10 If there are too many areas of potential trouble are you able to refuse the assignment?
11 Are you completely clear as to how the client will measure the success of the assignment?
12 Is your client fully committed to the project?

8   Delivering results for the client

There is nothing more difficult to take in hand, more perilous to conduct, or more uncertain in its success, than to take the lead in the introduction of a new order of things.

Nicolo Machiavelli, *The Prince*, 1532.

Getting a consultancy assignment done and done well can often be quite tricky. This chapter suggests some ideas to help you keep your clients happy.

8.1 IT consultancy assignments change

The result of a successful IT consulting assignment is that the client's business is in better condition than it was when the project commenced. This is achieved by the IT consultant delivering solutions to problems or helping clients take advantage of opportunities. It is about providing support for the business, which is not readily available internally. IT consulting assignments often involve working with some sort of change programme and these are often regarded as being some of the most difficult with which to succeed as they do not always have the wholehearted support of the individuals whose working lives are being changed. Furthermore these types of assignments often evolve or change themselves. You can begin with one set of objectives and quickly realize that you actually need to achieve something else. This can of course lead to both considerable opportunities as well as problems for the IT consultant. Thus delivering concrete results for the client, which the client actually appreciates as being of value, can often be quite a challenge.

What is actually needed?
There are several different challenges in establishing what the client actually needs and of course what the client actually needs may not be what the client wants. Sometimes the IT consultant will find him or herself caught between knowing what the client should do and having been given a specific job of work which is what the client wants. This is one of the many situations in which the IT consultant has to show a distinct penchant for diplomacy.

As mentioned before, consultancy work has to be done in such a way and at such a price that the client is convinced that he or she has obtained value for money. When expressed in this way it is obvious that from the client's perspective an IT consultancy project is an outsourcing arrangement whereby expertise or skills or a combination of both are being bought in to achieve a particular objective or a set of objectives. This being the case it is essential that the client play a central role in managing this consultancy process.[1] Unmanaged IT consultants will not often produce their full potential value. Of course, sometimes the client is so tied up with other business matters that the IT consultant may be left on his or her own for extended periods. If this is the case then both the client and the IT consultant will find it useful to have an agreed method of working on the project and an agreed method of managing the assignment as a whole. This needs to be clearly stated right up front if potential misunderstandings are to be avoided. The key issue is that both parties need to know exactly what is going on and how both sides view the progress of the assignment. It is also essential that if any changes to the project be suggested that these are discussed as early as possible.

8.2 Active benefit realization

One such method involves regular feedback sessions to ensure that the consultancy objectives remain relevant and that the work performed continues to move towards a satisfactory solution to the problems is referred to as Active Benefit Realization (ABR).

. . . ENSURE THAT THE CONSULTANCY OBJECTIVES REMAIN RELEVANT . . .

[1] If the client is indifferent to the IT consultancy project and refuses to play a central role in its planning and control then you should prepare yourself for problems. Consultants can seldom achieve real results on their own. They really do need the involvement of the client management and other members of staff.

ABR is an approach to project management and specifically to IT consultancy and development projects, which concentrates on achieving the maximum value from the project by focusing on the delivery of real business benefits. These benefits are achieved through a process of continuous involvement, in fact participation of both the IT consultants together with the client staff in achieving the project's objectives. This process relies on regular feedback and discussion of how the project is proceeding and whether the original objects of the project are still valid or relevant and is called continuous participative evaluation of the IT consulting assignment. ABR is an important approach to the management of IT consultancy assignments because it is relatively easy for such projects to stray off track.

ABR actually requires a partnership mind set whereby the IT consultant and the client see themselves working together to solve the problem or take advantage of the opportunity. ABR usually requires a broad focus on business issues underpinning the assignment, although the technical side of the project needs also to be carefully managed. This approach does not allow the client management to feel that the whole responsibility for the project rests with the IT consultants. Client management and the IT consultants are clearly jointly involved and they need to co-ensure both the success of the project and the delivery of benefits for the organization.

8.3 Formative evaluation

As the IT consultancy project develops the IT consultant and the clients who are the principal stakeholders acquire a more comprehensive understanding of the actual challenges or opportunities presented by the original problem. They will then jointly guide the assignment through a process referred to as formative evaluation towards a solution that delivers real improvements or benefits for the organization. Formative evaluation is concerned with keeping projects focused on benefits and thus avoiding waste of resources. The concept is central to ABR because formative evaluation is the vehicle for sustaining a dialogue between the IT consultant and the client management, which ensures the desired outcome of the project. At one level formative evaluation may be seen as a process whereby all the relevant stakeholders in the IT consultant project may contribute their views and values as to how

... REGULAR REVIEW MEETINGS ...

the assignment should proceed. This process requires regular review meetings during which an open attitude allows a comprehensive and meaningful discussion of all the key issues related to the assignment.

Formative evaluation provides a formal mechanism for improving project performance, which will take you through the whole duration of the project. Its objective is to improve project benefit delivery and ABR needs to be contrasted to those evaluations, which are done for the purpose of making basic decisions about whether or not the project has succeeded.[2]

The partnership mind set

It is actually very difficult for an IT consultant to achieve a partnership mind set with a client. The IT consultant is always an outsider (even if they have been working there for quite a long time) and there will inevitably be a degree of suspicion of the consultant's motives and possibly also a degree of jealousy. However, the only way to achieve the partnership mind set is to put time into understanding the client organization thoroughly and also the personal aspirations and ambitions of the client manager with whom you are working. This is both difficult and time consuming but it can actually be a critical success factor for your project.

The term formative is taken from the word *form*, 'to mould by discipline and education'. Formative evaluation is viewed as a reiterative evaluation and decision-making process continually influencing the project and influencing the participants, with the overall objective to achieve more beneficial outcomes from the project. Because of its ongoing nature, which relies on evaluation continuous feedback, formative evaluation is sometimes referred to as learning evaluation which highlights that both the client and the IT consultant often need to learn what are the real needs of the organization.

8.4 Welcome change suggestions

To be successful with formative evaluation it is necessary to establish a mind set, which welcomes suggestions of possible

[2] Evaluations conducted for the purpose of making decisions about whether or not the project has succeeded are referred to as summative evaluations. The term summative evaluation is derived from the word *sum* and is viewed as an act of evaluation assessing the final (sum) impact of a project or an investment. Summative evaluation normally focuses on a brief answer, which is that the project has either succeeded or failed. Formative evaluation gives a longer response as to how to proceed to ensure the successful delivery of benefits.

change. It is also most important that there is no attempt to limit the source of such suggestions to executives only. The views of all competent stakeholders[3] should be carefully listened to. Sometimes formative evaluation is referred to as learning evaluation as its intent is to improve performance and thus achieve a more satisfactory outcome.

8.5 Financial implications

Sometimes the ABR approach throws up the need for material changes to the IT consultancy assignments. It is usually much better to know about this during the assignment rather than at the end when it may be too late to do anything about the situation. However, sometimes these changes mean that the IT

... CHANGES MEAN THAT THE IT CONSULTANT WILL HAVE TO DO EXTRA WORK ...

consultant will have to do extra work and the question, which always arises, is who will pay for this. If the IT consultancy assignment is on a time and materials basis then there is normally no problem. However, if there is a fixed price associated with the work then it may be necessary to negotiate a new price for the work. If the changes are necessary to accommodate new business circumstances there is usually no problem with this.

8.6 Complements traditional project management

This ABR process complements traditional project management and financial management techniques that are necessary to ensure sound management practice for successfully delivering an IT consultancy outcome. Thus to be successful you will also need to use the standard project management techniques a number of which were discussed in the previous chapter.

Delivering real benefits for clients is not a trivial issue. IT consultancy projects can and do go wrong. As an IT consultant you just cannot assume that because you have a signed contract

---

[3] It is a considerable challenge to all consultants to know who are the most competent or the most knowledgeable individuals in the client firm. There is often an unfortunate assumption that the more senior the person the more competent and knowledgeable he or she is. This is clearly not always true but it can be difficult to be seen taking the word of someone junior before his or her superiors.

you actually know exactly what is needed and what will be acceptable. There can be a difference between what the client wants and what is truly needed by the organization and bringing these two together can be problematical.[4] You need to continuously check that the project is on track. In this respect perceptions count for much more than any 'reality'. In fact some would argue that the only reality is perception. It is always very important to remember that beauty, contact lenses and your competence are all in the eye of the beholder. If for whatever reason your client does not think that you are delivering benefit then you will not be seen as value for money. The value for money proposition is what underpins successful IT consulting and if your client is unconvinced about this then no matter how clever your work has been it is unlikely that your project will be considered a success.[5]

The techniques described in this chapter will help you make sure that this does not happen and that the client feels satisfied with the result of the assignment.

8.7 Summary and conclusion

Don't underestimate the difficulty in achieving a successful outcome to an IT consultancy assignment. To succeed you need to stay close to the client and to understand how his or her requirements change during the course of the project. This chapter suggests a technique called Active Benefit Realization to

---

[4] The potential gap between what the client wants and what the organization may actually need is a dilemma that IT consultants have to face from time to time. There is no easy answer as to what to do if this gap appears. Less experienced consultants will argue that you should actively point out to the client that he or she has not really understood the situation and that you can achieve better results if the client follows the consultant's advice, i.e. interpretation of the situation. More cynical consultants will simply say 'just do what the client wants as he who pays the piper calls the tune'. Others will try to compromise and suggest that it is often useful to debate the difference between what is wanted and what might be needed and try to find a middle course. I would always favour some discussion on this issue but from practice I have personally found that the client often knows just what he or she wants and the consultant's suggestion that something else is needed is often not very welcome. This is always a very challenging area.

[5] The value for money issue will raise its head again and again. This is because consultants were generally and naturally more expensive than full-time members of staff. This will inevitably be the case, as consultants always have to pay much of their own expenses that the firm pay out invisibly for the full-time member of staff. And many organizations worry about the fact that larger sums are paid to consultants.

help you with this. For a full account of Active Benefit Realization see *Achieving Maximum Value from your Information Systems – A Process Approach* by Dan Remenyi, Michael Sherwood-Smith with Terry White published by John Wiley and Sons. The full reference is given in the reading list (Appendix A).

8.8 Checklist

Things to think about when delivering results for the client

1 Have you listed all the deliverables as stated in the contract?
2 Are there any other deliverables that are required but not specifically mentioned?
3 Do you know precisely when these are required?
4 Have you told your client about Active Benefit Realization and Formative Evaluation?
5 Have you established an understanding with your client as to how you will handle any changes to the contract?
6 Have you discussed how changes will be charged?

Finding the next client

The world that we have made as a result of the level of thinking we have done thus far creates problems that we cannot solve at the same levels as they were created.

Attributed to Albert Einstein by Pascale, R., *Managing on the Edge*, Penguin Books, London, 1990, p. 11.

Every year hundreds or maybe thousands of IT professionals decide to give up their full-time permanent jobs and start their own IT consultancy. Many succeed in getting their consultancy business going by finding a few clients and doing some interesting and reasonably well-remunerated work. This will usually be exciting and fun. They will feel satisfied that they will have broken away from being a cog in the corporate world to doing their own thing. They may be working harder and longer hours but they will be doing this for themselves and that will bring with it a lot of satisfaction.

Getting to this point is a very useful start, but it is quite another matter to convert a few consulting jobs into what might be considered to be a sustainable IT consulting business. The former may not have been that difficult, but the latter is a major challenge. It is for this reason that not many attempts to set up an IT consultancy business survive. Most IT consultancy start-ups last no longer than a few years, after which their founder returns to a job in a large organization again or does something else.

Consultancy contracts are a transitory business. By their very nature most consultancy assignments have a limited duration. Some may only be days long, others weeks or maybe months. Very occasionally you might even find a consultancy job that will run for a year of two, but that is quite rare in the field of IT consultancy. If the organization has a big enough problem or a long-term problem they don't usually try to solve this situation by employing a consultant. It is more common for them to simply go out and recruit an individual to their staff.

The short-term nature of IT consultancy assignments presents a special problem, especially to those consultants who are working entirely on their own. This is to do with how you find the next job or the next client while being fully committed to giving your full attention to the current job. This is a problem for all consultancy firms, large and small, and there is no easy answer to the question. Some IT consultants ignore the problem of the next client until the current job is complete. In fact your daily rate should be adequate to give you enough money to take a short catch-up break between jobs during which you update yourself if you need to and find your next piece of work. However, this approach can sometimes lead to long periods between jobs, which can be very unpleasant especially if your resources are not too substantial.

Of course if you have a partner or you are in a strategic alliance with some organization then the problem of the next job might entirely go away or at least be significantly reduced. Your partner can be looking for the next job while you are fully occupied with the current one. Or your strategic ally can be lining up opportunities for you to follow up as soon as you have a free moment.

You can also employ a sales person. You may be lucky and find someone who is good and who is prepared to work mainly on commission. But this is rare. Sales people are intrinsically expensive and although they can be very helpful indeed, it is generally considered that in the field of IT consultancy, in the final analysis, new work can only be sold by the actual consultant. Although it is clear that this is not always true there is no doubt a substantial element of truth in this proposition.

Thus the finding of the next client is not a trivial exercise and if you want to work entirely on your own, you need to face this significant challenge square on.

Here are some suggestions that you might find helpful.

. . . A SET AMOUNT OF TIME FOR MARKETING EACH WEEK

It was mentioned in the Chapter 3 on **Setting up your IT consultancy business** that in your planning you might consider putting aside a set amount of time for marketing each week. When you first start out if you are not able to line up a client to start work with as soon as you leave your old job, you will of course have been spending all your time marketing. You will have made many contacts, some of which will have shown some interest in you. You may actually have some work proposals still out with potential clients awaiting decisions. Decisions to employ consultants can take a long time and until a proposal has been formally refused or rejected you should always consider it as a potential next client. Remember, what is high on your agenda may not be high on your client's agenda. The task is, without annoying your client, to ensure that these potential suppliers of work do not lose interest in you or, worse, entirely forget about your existence. Thus one of the central issues is maintaining contact and making sure that you have some visibility in the market place.[1]

Visibility in the market place can come from several different sources. The following are the most important ones readily available to the start-up IT consultancy:

1 Making and maintaining personal contacts.
2 Joining a group such as the Computer Society, the Chamber of Commerce, etc.
3 Placing your name on a Web list
4 Speaking at conferences and seminars.
5 Writing for the press.
6 Writing a book.
7 Playing a role in the community.

9.1 Making and maintaining personal contact

There are numerous ways of keeping contact and the way you choose will depend upon how you made the contact to begin

---

[1] This point is to some extent controversial. Some business consultancy firms have rules for their sales staff which require them to close a deal with a potential client within, say, three months of any contact with them. If the sales person does not make a sale within this period the management of the business consultancy firm will insist that the sales person drops the potential client from their list and does not spend any more time trying to sell to them. This is probably too harsh an approach to filtering out low potential sales prospects for the newly started-up IT consultancy.

with and your style of running your business. You may have made a lot of contacts over the past few years and you may have to decide which of these are likely to be the best prospects for future work. Thus having prioritized your contacts you might just make regular phone calls, say once a month or once a quarter. You might just pay the prospect a visit to see if they still have a problem with which you could be of help. You might visit to update them on a new approach to an aspect of IT you have come up with. Each consultancy job that you do should be a learning experience for you. So towards the end of each job you should have something new to offer your prospective clients.

The main point here is to keep talking to your contacts and that you expand what you can offer them provided the new offering truly falls within your competencies.

You might develop a newsletter to send to your contacts or prospects. This might be a paper-based document or it might be produced electronically and despatched or circulated on the Internet. However, you need to be aware that there are a large number of newsletters circulating and that you will have to work quite hard to make yours sufficiently novel and interesting to read. Otherwise this will be a waste of effort.

... YOU MIGHT INVITE THEM TO LUNCH OR FOR AN OCCASIONAL DRINK AFTER WORK

If you are on friendly terms with your business prospects you might invite them to lunch or for an occasional drink after work.

9.2 Joining a group such as the Computer Society

Becoming a member of a society or a group such as the Computer Society or the Chamber of Commerce will give you visibility. These contacts are not likely to produce business in the short term but they can in the medium to longer term help you meet appropriate people and this can lead to business.

9.3 Placing your name on a Web list

There are a variety of Web lists of IT consultants on which you may place your name and which will produce some leads from time to time.

9.4 Speaking at conferences and seminars

As an IT consultant you may feel that you have some new leading edge concept that you wish to draw to the attention of your prospects and if this is the case you can organize an executive briefing or even a seminar. It is possible to do this on your own by hiring a room in a hotel or at a conference centre but it can also be effective to do this in conjunction with one of the IT professional societies or a Chamber of Commerce. There are also professional conference and seminar organizers to whom you could offer your services. You might even find it useful to obtain a small part-time role at a local college or university where you might meet mature students who could be looking for help with problems at work.

Preparing to present a paper at a conference or deliver a seminar does take a considerable amount of work so you need to be reasonably confident that you will obtain the right visibility and perhaps a reasonable fee before embarking on this type of promotion venture.

. . . BE REASONABLY CONFIDENT THAT YOU WILL OBTAIN THE RIGHT VISIBILITY . . .

If you are good at this then you could make presenting at conferences and seminars a specific line of business, which can be quite lucrative.

9.5 Writing for the press

Newspapers and magazines are in continual need of new stories or new angles on old ones. And another useful way of keeping your name visible is to write articles and have them published either in the general press or in some specialized newspaper or magazine. If you can arrange to have your ideas published in a suitable newspaper then you can sometimes receive a considerable amount of interest and attention. However, this will not happen with every newspaper and sometimes this type of writing can become more effort than it is worth.[2]

The idea of writing for visibility may be extended to the Internet where, as mentioned above, an increasing number of IT

[2] Some newspapers sometimes have trouble in filling all their pages, i.e. they have unused space which is called white space. When this occurs they look around for articles that they can use. It can be helpful if you can make contact with such a newspaper and agree that they will publish articles for you. However, if you do not get some enquiries as a result of this press exposure then you may not want to persevere with it as it does take time to write these articles.

consultants have their own newsletter. Sometimes these Internet newsletters are complemented with or by a discussion group which is also a useful tool for ensuring a degree of visibility. The Internet and the Web are indeed powerful ways of keeping in touch and ensuring your visibility but they suffer from the major drawback that you can attract a considerable amount of attention from individuals and organizations who can consume much of your time and have no intention or no ability to offer you any paid work. It is hard to assess who could be of importance to your business through Internet or Web contact so just be careful that you don't spend too much time on this activity.

9.6 Writing a book

WRITING A BOOK IS NOT, FOR MOST IT CONSULTANTS, A SHORT PROJECT . . .

Although this is no easy matter, if you have something interesting to say writing a book can be useful to the IT consultant and can resulted in a considerable amount of business. Writing a book is not, for most IT consultants, a short project and if done on a part-time basis can take many months or even years to complete. Do not begin writing your book until you have a plan as to how it will be published, even if it is only that you will publish it yourself. There is no great problem in having one hundred copies printed and you could use these as a way of catching the attention of prospects.

Writing a book can result in obtaining very interesting work. But do bear in mind that not every book written by a consultant has led to work. In my case only one of my several books actually resulted in consultancy, but it has produced a number of very important jobs for me over the years.

9.7 Playing a role in the community

An IT consultant can make him or herself visible by offering to help out at the local school or through the parish council or through the local boy scouts or girl guides associations. IT know-how is always in short supply and by making yourself useful your name will get around. Joining your local Rotary or Round Table club is another way of gaining exposure. It is probably a good idea first to check out who the other members of these groups are to see if there might be some useful contact there.

There are two more important ways that an IT consultant can set about finding the next client while still relatively busy with the current assignment:

1 Looking for more work with an existing client.
2 Have your client recommend you to suppliers and/or clients.

9.8 Looking for more work with an existing client

Existing clients are often an excellent source of new business. You should be close to your clients and you should know not only what their current needs are but also what their future needs are likely to be. Furthermore you should also know how best to sell to them.

You may be able to sell on from your current project to the next phase in that work or you may be able to sell an entirely different type of job.

If you can expand the job you are doing to cover a wider field then you may be able to generate sufficient work for you to be able to recruit another member of staff. Of course this work would have to be sustainable for a while to justify employing an extra pair of hands.

9.9 Have your client recommend you to suppliers and/or clients

While working with your existing client you will invariably meet some of their suppliers and/or clients as well as perhaps other consultants. All these people may be regarded as potential clients for you or at least good prospects for your own network.

In some cases it may even be appropriate for your current client to recommend you to one of their customers or suppliers especially if you have been working on a system that involves interfacing with your clients' customers or suppliers. If such an opportunity exists it's important not to miss it.

As mentioned above it is not a trivial matter to find your next client. If it were, IT consulting would be a cinch and it's not. You always have to be on the lookout for business and this can be a very tiring process. However, over time as you become more established business begins to come to you. However, even in the most established IT consulting groups this can never be taken for granted.

9.10 Remember what the Internet can do for you

THE INTERNET IS ALSO AVAILABLE TO YOU TO LOOK FOR CLIENTS . . .

As a global directory the Internet allows the world to have access to the information that you decide to post on your website. Thus at the end of each job you need to update your CV by adding to the list of your work experience. If your last client will allow you to mention their name this can be helpful especially if they are a well-known organization. Then e-mail all your relevant prospects with this update on your service range. The Internet is also available to you to look for clients and you can find out much from a website about a prospect before you make any formal approach. This is invaluable in helping you refine what your offering is going to be.

9.11 Final note

The problem of finding the next client never goes away. Even long-standing, well-established consultants often find themselves wondering where the next job will come from. It is in the very nature of the consulting business and if you find this too distressful then IT consulting may not be for you. On the other hand this uncertainty is one of the things that makes working as a consultant challenging, exciting, sometimes miserable but never ever dull or boring.

9.12 Summary and conclusion

The three most important issues in running your own IT consultancy are marketing, marketing and marketing. Of course this does presume that you are basically competent and that you have skills that the market wants. After your basic competence and your marketable skills in IT then the overriding issue for a sustainable business is your ability to market yourself. This chapter provided some suggestions as to how you might be able to market yourself on an ongoing basis.

If you are going to succeed you will always have to keep the marketing issue at the forefront of your mind.

9.13 Checklist

Things to think about when working on finding the next client

1 Do you have any assignment proposals that are still in front of potential clients?

2 Have you acquired new skills from your current assignment that you would be able to offer to new prospective clients?

3 If your assignment proposal is older than three months contact the potential client and see if they are interested to have a revised proposal.

4 Have you prioritized your list of business contacts by whom is most likely to offer you an assignment?

5 Phone the three most probable potential clients and seek an appointment to discuss what you can do for them.

6 Have you attempted to sell on to your current client directly or to some other part of that organization?

7 Will your client allow you to write up your work as a case study and have it published in a professional journal or industry newspaper?

8 Have you made any interesting contacts with your current clients' suppliers or customers that you could follow up?

9 Do you have an arrangement with a local newspaper or journal to write occasional articles for them?

10 Have you discussed delivering or contributing to a seminar with your Chamber of Commerce or some other professional training provider?

10 Consulting and finding a product to sell

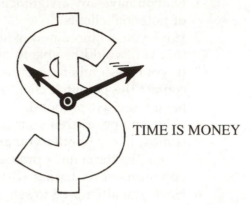

TIME IS MONEY

Anyone that tells you it is easy to change the way groups do things is either a liar, a management consultant or both. Change is hard for individuals; for groups it is next to impossible.

The Economist, June 1990.

When consultants get together they will often talk about the limitations they suffer by only having their time to sell. It is sometimes seen as a major concern as it definitely limits their potential income.

10.1 Making money as an IT consultant

Of course the profession of IT consulting can be a rewarding one. As well as having a challenging and highly satisfying job it is certainly possible for you to make a considerable amount of money. It is quite hard to put a number to these potential earnings, but I have occasionally heard about the IT consultant who has made a quarter of a million or even half a million pounds sterling a year. Every now and again one hears of the IT consultant billing a million pounds in a year. This type of income takes some earning and is made only after the IT consultant is very well established in the field as a world authority and it may take you a few years to get to this stage.

While this sort of financial success is impressive it is nonetheless not in the same sort of financial league that success in commerce or industry can lead to. Making and selling the right product or having the right chain of shops or the right transport company, to mention only three examples, can lead the successful entrepreneur to earn tens if not hundreds of millions of pounds. In commerce or industry there is no limit to the possible financial earnings of a really successful player. This is not really achievable by the IT consultant. The point is that IT consultants sell their time and there is a definite and finite limit to the number of hours or days an IT consultant can work in any one given year. Thus working for 48 weeks a year for 3 days every week a consultant charging £2,000 per day could bill £288,000. This would imply a 66% utilization of capacity, which is for many consultants, especially those asking £2,000 per day, quite a high rate. Nonetheless for a highly successful consultant this is perfectly achievable. But £288,000 is not millions of pounds.

10.2 Growing your business

Of course an IT consultant could grow his or her business practice and in time employ extra hands. Over a few years maybe 10 or 20 or even 100 consultants could be employed. If this size of business is achieved then large sums of money rising to millions of pounds can indeed be billed and if adequate cost controls are implemented large sums of money can be made. But this doesn't happen all that often in the IT consulting world.

Furthermore, if a large firm is developed the IT consultant may be able to sell the business as a going concern for a sizable sum of money. During the past few years, with the stock market racing ahead, IT and other business consultancies were sold for huge prices, in some cases hundreds of millions of pounds, but this was probably as much due to the e-bubble as to the intrinsic worth of the consulting businesses themselves.

... THE IT CONSULTANT CAN DIVERSIFY BY SELLING A PRODUCT

Besides the sale of standard consulting services the IT consultant can diversify by selling a product. Having a suitable product for sale is one of the ways in which an IT consultant can quickly grow the business. However, it is not an easy matter to find a suitable product. In fact it is sometimes regarded as the holy grail of the consulting business to have a marketable product to sell. The logic of having a product to sell is that there is no theoretical limit to the number of units that can be sold and thus there is no practical maximum the consultant can earn.

However, finding a suitable or appropriate product, which they are comfortable to sell, is for many consultants a major challenge. In the first instance many IT consultants do not feel that selling a product is compatible with a professional services business and indeed this may well be the case.[1] Offering advice on IT strategy and at the same time being able to supply laser printers may not make the impression that is required to succeed with either of these enterprises. Certainly it would be ethically questionable if you were to hold yourself out as an independent computer vendor selection consultant while at the same time obtaining a fee or a commission for a hardware or software vendor.

10.3 The independent consultant

However, some IT consultants do not pretend to be independent. Some will say that they are consultants with expertise in a particular project management software application package. Thus when they give advice on project management issues they will do so bearing in mind that they know one software application package really well and that they can operationalize their advice most effectively through the use of that program. Others will have the same sort of approach but through the use of some hardware product or a combination of hardware and software.

If as an IT consultant you are involved with a hardware or software vendor and you don't want to be criticized for having mixed loyalties or conflicting objectives then it is really important that you make this clear right up front when approaching a client. However, once that is done then there is generally no problem in combining your sales and consulting skills. Some IT consulting firms have done this especially well and made very substantial sums of money out of it. By the way, there is no reason to be associated with only one product. Some consultants will have a portfolio of hardware and software with which they are associated.

---

[1] Of course for most people this does depend on the precise nature of the consultancy and the type of product concerned.

10.4 Develop a product

A variation of this is when the IT consultancy develops its own product. For example, this product could be a piece of application software or it could be a systems development methodology. In either case to use it in order to leverage the consultant's income it would have to be available for operation independent of the consultant him or herself. Ideally this product needs to be sold with all the necessary documentation so that the user can operate it without too much ongoing assistance. Of course it would indeed be useful if as well as the product itself the IT consultancy were able to sell training for the use of the product. If this could be licensed to independent trainers then another stream in income could be enjoyed. What is now being described is a hybrid business consisting of consulting, software sales and training.

IF YOU DECIDE TO DEVELOP A SOFTWARE PRODUCT . . .

If you decide to develop a software product such as this you need to pay careful attention to the costs of creating and marketing the product. The economics of product development can be quite challenging. Although the unit cost of reproducing the product will probably be very little indeed, the initial costs of setting this venture up can be substantial. You will probably have to move a material number of products to make any money out of such a scheme. It can easily cost tens if not hundreds of thousands of pounds to produce a software product to the high quality necessary for it to be sold in the current market place. Gone are the days when something could be cobbled together and sold without being professionally produced, tested and packaged. There are not many small independent IT consultancies that can really afford this type of development investment.

There is, however, a halfway house with some of the characteristics of a product, but which is not directly tied to a hardware or software product or vendor. This is the arena of the seminar. Many IT consultants offer seminars. Sometimes these seminars are skills oriented such as How to do Financial Planning with a Spreadsheet. Or the seminars may be of a more general educational variety such as How to Select Appropriate Software for the Marketing Department.

The economics of seminars is quite interesting. If you really know your subject well – off by heart so to speak – and if you are a competent public speaker and you have a natural instinct for teaching, then you will probably be able to put a one- or even a two-day seminar together with little or no effort over a couple of days. If this were the case then from a financial point of view you would have, say, only two days effort to recover. On the other hand if you are not quite so expert or versatile and you need to do research and if you need to practise delivery and perhaps spend a lot of time working out how to present the material then developing a seminar might be too expensive and perhaps not really such a good idea for you.

Seminars can be run in a local hotel or you can even hire a room out of academic term in a local university. You can run them on your own or you can invite others to speak with you. It is often useful to combine some theory with a session from someone who has just done the work and can therefore explain the practical problems. If you are in the vendor selection end of the IT consulting business and you want to make money out of seminars and in addition sell more vendor selection assignments you might hold a seminar on this subject and invite a satisfied client of yours to speak at the event with you. It is always important to charge attendees for these seminars. If you don't you will obtain a low rate of turnout on the day and may be stuck with a lot of seminar overhead costs and virtually no audience at all.

Although such events are not easy to market those who make a success of them earn both a return on the seminar and at the same time the possibility to pitch for new business to some of the seminar attendees.

Other types of products that consultants sometimes sell are books or research reports. There are a wide variety of options here. Sometimes IT consultants will write their own books, which may be published by a well-known reputable publisher. On other occasions vanity publishers are used. Here the author or in this case the consultant will usually be paid for the book to be published. In either case the IT consultant will be using the book to generate a small amount of revenue and also obtain more business.

... THE MOST EFFECTIVE WAY OF FINDING SUCH A PRODUCT IS TO ATTEND THE TRADE EXHIBITIONS

If you are thinking of finding a product to supplement your IT consultancy business and you don't have the funds to develop one yourself then the most effective way of finding such a product is to attend the trade exhibitions. There are dozens of these every year in the United Kingdom and their time and location may be easily found on the Web. Of course there is a much larger variety of such products exhibited at similar industry shows in the USA.

10.5 Summary and conclusion

Nearly all IT consultants would like to find a product to sell. However, it is not easy to find a suitable product and not many consultants ever achieve this. Therefore do not spend too much time on this issue. But on the other hand if an interesting product comes your way which complements the main thrust of your IT consulting business then perhaps you should give it some attention.

10.6 Checklist

Things to think about when finding a product to sell

1 Try to find a product that will complement your consulting services.
2 Be careful that neither the development nor the production of the product detracts from your ability to deliver the consulting work.
3 If you decide to market a product make sure you have a reasonable balance between the two parts of your business.
4 Be aware that there could be conflicts of interests between acting as a consultant and your selling your product.

11

Keep your eye on the ball

An expert is a man who has made all mistakes, which can be made, in a very narrow field.

Niels Henrik David Bohr, 10 November 1972.

To ensure medium to long-term success with your IT consulting business you will need to keep an eye on a number of critical issues that can cause business failure. These issues will persist over the life of your business and if you at any stage forget them you might find that your business will be quite quickly in trouble.

In this chapter I present five important issues. This is not intended to be a definitive list, but rather five of the more common difficulties start-up IT consultants find themselves in.

11.1 Business cycles

Just about every organization experiences some form of business cycle. In some cases the cycle can be very short term such as restaurants that are packed out every Saturday night and empty on Mondays. Other businesses have a once a month cycle such as those that get a boost to trade when the monthly pay check arrives on employees' desks.

IT consulting also has cycles, which are more closely related to the general success of the economy than anything else. And as you will know the UK economy has been expanding and contracting over the past few years. As a result some IT consultancies have had to cope with increases and then decreases in demand.

The expansion–contraction model

A consultant I knew ran his business on the expansion–contraction model. He always seemed to have enough business to keep five or six people well occupied. However, he would take on extra business and allow his team to grow to 12 or 15 people when the demand was there for their services. The problem was that he did not seem able to sustain that level of business as he was not prepared to put enough resources into marketing.

Subcontracting to friends

Be especially careful about subcontracting work to friends. The business of an IT consultant I knew grew much more quickly than he could cope with. So he subcontracted part of an important assignment to a friend. For whatever reason this part of the assignment did not work out well with the client complaining about the quality of the friend's work. The end result was that the IT consultant had to fire his friend, pay back fees to the client and did not get the extension to the assignment he was hoping to. It was just bad news all round.

Also there is the fact that IT consultancy can be 'lumpy'. For example, I obtained a contract a few years ago for which I needed five extra pairs of hands for six months. A newcomer to the business of IT consulting could have gone out and recruited more people. I actually found individuals who would work for me on contract which was of course more expensive than hiring regular staff. But when the job was over there were no redundancy problems.

The problem really arises when you think that you have a permanent increase in business activity and you hire a half dozen new people and you lease motor cars for them and you acquire additional office space. If it transpires that this new level of business is not sustainable due to a change in the business cycle or for that matter for any other reason you can be in real trouble. This is the problem of expanding too quickly. And it is often almost impossible to know when the business opportunity presents itself to you if it's only temporary or if it is a really sustainable increase in business level. The cost of downsizing can be really expensive and it's not just the actual redundancy money. The hidden cost is the impact on your own morale and the morale of the others who are left after the downsizing exercise. But in the end the payment to the people involved will often be less than the payments associated in getting out of the leases – if you can get out of the leases. Sometimes

THE COST OF DOWNSIZING CAN BE REALLY EXPENSIVE . . .

you just won't be able to break the lease and you will be faced with having to try to find another tenant or sell the vehicles and take whatever losses there are associated with that.

An important thought that all start-up consultants should constantly keep in mind is that one of the greatest causes of failure is success, i.e. premature overexpansion or being caught by a contraction in the business cycle.

11.2 Fixed priced jobs can be undercosted

As an IT consultant you will be frequently requested to quote for an assignment on a fixed price basis. This is not in itself unreasonable as your prospective client will want to know how much he or she is letting their organization in for. However, many IT consultancy jobs are really intrinsically difficult to cost estimate. Every experienced IT consultant will tell you tales of the job that was underquoted. Sometimes these jobs were not underquoted by 10 or 20 or even 50% but by 500%. If you are in a really bad situation you may have to walk away from a job and see if the client will actually sue you. But this seldom happens, especially if the cost runaway occurs when the job is well on its way. The client may then be committed and if you are not paid enough to keep you going then the client will lose the whole job.

> **Avoid disputes where at all possible**
>
> When you are a small start-up IT consulting business it is important to be on good terms not only with your clients but also with your suppliers and subcontractors. A consultant I know had a very unpleasant row with a book publisher about a relatively small account. In the end the IT consultant paid up begrudgingly. The book publisher was so annoyed that he made sure that whenever he could he told people about how unreliable the IT consultant was. In the end the IT consultant lost an important opportunity because of this rather silly row.

There is no doubt that in IT consulting you can count on everything costing twice as much as you initially think and that jobs will take twice as long as you originally estimated. One way of protecting yourself against cost runaways is to quote for jobs in phases and then negotiate the cost changes as you proceed. This is not necessarily an easy strategy to sell to a prospective client.

One small thing you can do to help protect yourself against rising costs is to time stamp your proposals with conditions such as this fixed price will only be valid for, say, 30 or 60 days.

... STAMP YOUR PROPOSALS WITH CONDITIONS ...

An important corollary of this, which has already been mentioned, is that it is possible to 'buy' the business by undercharging. This strategy is frequently regretted so it is probably just as well to avoid it.

11.3 Losing control over cash flow

Many business schools teach students in the first few months of their business course that cash is ultimately more important than profit. This truism is based on the fact that many businesses that are insolvent and are thus wound up are actually showing profits in their income statements and balance sheets.

The critical point is to realize that profit is a notional difference between income and costs, where at least some of the costs are to do with subjective evaluations of assets. Cash is to do with how many notes and coins your bankers will hand over to you if you pitch up at your bank and ask for your money. There is nothing notional about cash.

It thus follows that you can't pay your bills with profit.

And if you can't pay your bills you are insolvent and by law you have to close down.

. . . YOU MAY HAVE TO PLAY A BALANCING ACT . . .

To make sure that you always have enough cash is one of the primary objectives. To ensure this you may have to play a balancing act between paying what you owe and receiving what is owed to you. The bigger you get the more difficult this becomes. Most of your costs will be staff related, i.e. either payroll or subcontractors' costs. You have to meet these every month. Sometimes your clients will keep you waiting 60, 90 or what my old accounting teacher used to call one hundred and plenty days. When this happens you can easily run out of cash and find yourself in trouble, and if you go to the bank you may not find a very welcoming reception. Banks do not like to lend money to anyone in a crisis. The way banks think is that you need to forecast your cash requirements six or even 12 months ahead and negotiate facilities well in advance. In this respect they are probably quite right.

11.4 The flavour of the month or of the year

Some businesses are very stable. There are business lines for which there is virtually constant demand. Such businesses include basic foodstuffs, essential transport, medical services and supplies to mention only a few. Other businesses are much more volatile and depend on swings in the market. The classic example of this is the fashion industry where one year skirts are short and in the next year they are long. One year lipstick is scarlet red and the next year peach pink! In fashion related industries much more effort has to be focused in anticipating how the market will move.

Certain aspects of IT consulting can be seen as relating to fashion. One year client–server architecture is the only show in town. The next year it is Web enabled interfaces and so on. For the IT consultant, adapting services is a continual challenge. You have to continually monitor your market place and understand how it is shifting. The IT consultant is in a continuous state of learning. No sooner has one set of competencies been settled than another set needs to be learnt.

Of course the key to real success is being able to anticipate movements in the market. If you can foresee a trend and be ready just as it becomes the most sought-after skill then you have a significant competitive advantage. However, as the wise man once said 'Predictions are difficult – especially those about the future!'

11.5 Not understanding the risk facing your organization

In general it takes time for many new entrepreneurs to understand the issue of risk. In a previous chapter I discussed project risk. This is usually straightforward and if given sufficient attention it should be controllable.

The risk referred to here is a more general one. Business school students are taught that there are two types of risk that any organization faces. The first of these is to do with the nature of the type of business and this has been discussed under section 11.4, 'The flavour of the month or of the year'. From this it is hoped that you will agree that the business risk of an IT consultancy is relatively high.

Bad debts

An issue of continuous importance to all IT consultants is that of bad debts. The assignment isn't complete until the money is in the bank. Unfortunately everyone will at sometime face a client whose financial status is weak and it is critical to approach such a situation with a lot of care. Over the years I have known a few consultants who have not been careful about this. One of them extended a large amount of credit to a client who then went into liquidation and whose creditors received nothing. This bad debt in turn caused the IT consultant to go broke.

The second type of risk is to do with how much money you have had to borrow. As mentioned in an earlier chapter there are several ways in which you could have borrowed money such as by obtaining an overdraft or by leasing to mention only two. If your business has been fully financed by yourself and you do not have any bank overdraft or you haven't had to lease any equipment then it is said that you have very little financial risk exposure. On the other hand if you have a big overdraft and several big leases you may well have substantial financial risk exposure.

As an IT consultancy will inevitably have a reasonably high business risk it is important that you do not take in too much financial risk as well.

11.6 The great tax surprise

Sometimes tax bills can come as a surprise and start-up IT consultants can be embarrassed when the time comes to pay their tax. There are a variety of taxes that have to be paid and the one that can really present problems is the VAT. The only sensible attitude to VAT is that you are collecting tax on behalf of the government. This money does not belong to you or your business. You have to account for every penny of it and you have to have the money on hand precisely when it is due. Getting into difficulties with the VAT man is something that you really must avoid.

. . . YOU HAVE TO HAVE THE MONEY ON HAND PRECISELY WHEN IT IS DUE

Of course the same can be said for all other taxes. PAYE generally doesn't cause many problems as we have all been disciplined from our first day at work that we have to 'pay as you earn'. But with your own business you will have to follow a different tax regime and it is money well spent to have an accountant help you with this. If you get a corporation tax bill or a VAT tax bill out of the blue for which you don't have the money, it can certainly cause your business great difficulty if it doesn't actually put it under.

11.7 Summary and conclusion

The task of running a business is never finished. Every day new challenges arrive and new decisions have to be made. Those who are good at understanding the environment in which they are running their business and who are also aware of the different types of risk they face have a better chance of coping. This chapter offered you an opportunity to sensitize yourself to some of the more common mistakes I have seen IT consultants make.

12

Minding your own business

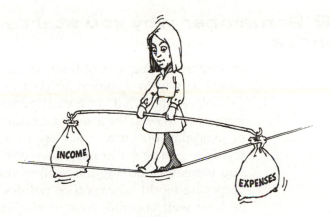

Annual income twenty pounds, annual expenditure nineteen nineteen and six, result happiness. Annual income twenty pounds, annual expenditure twenty pounds ought and six, result misery.

Dickens, C., *David Copperfield*, spoken by Mr Micawber and first published in 1850, p. 209: Centennial Edition, 1950.

12.1 Keeping your business going is the real challenge

It is only when you are up and running as an IT consultant that the real challenges and perhaps the real 'fun' begins. It might or might not be difficult to start up your IT consultancy business, but it is certainly a full-time job to keep it going. Most IT consultancies simply do not last. Failure occurs for one or more of many reasons, even after the business has been established and is up and running. As long as you want to remain an IT consultant working for yourself you will need to continuously have your eye on the ball.

There is no doubt that creating an IT consulting business is clearly a substantial feat. However, having done this the real challenge is in growing the business and keeping it going year after year. A sustainable business in the medium to long term is the real objective. To achieve this you will not only need to be an excellent IT consultant, but you will also need to have both business sense and also be well equipped with general management skills. There are in fact few businesses that are quite as demanding as running an IT consultancy[1] and you will need to think carefully as to how you want to sustain and grow your business.

12.2 Remember why you started your own business

In understanding the options available to you it is useful to reflect on why you started up your IT consulting business in the first place, and what were your personal objectives. It is always important to keep these in mind because in the hustle and bustle of everyday business it is easy to lose sight of what you are trying to achieve. You may have got into this business because you were not enjoying the routine and the regimentation of the corporate world where office politics was at least as important as how well you did your work. You may have got into this business because you felt that you were not being properly remunerated for the contribution you were making to your organization. You may have got into this business because you saw that promotion was not going to come your way until your boss retired or was run over by the proverbial no. 42 bus. Not seeing a clear career path leading to an interesting and lucrative job is one of the most popular reasons for setting up one's own business. You may have got into this business because you had been fired or maybe your previous employers were polite enough to allow you to resign – maybe you made a mistake or maybe you were just too entrepreneurial for them. You may have got into this business because you mistakenly thought that by working for yourself you were going to have lashings of free time to pursue your numerous interests and hobbies.

So the way that you will sustain and grow your IT consulting business will depend on where you have come from. If you got into this business because you felt that you were not being properly remunerated or because you were just too entrepreneurial for your previous employer you will probably be keen to grow your business as fast as possible. On the other hand if it was because you felt that you were not enjoying the routine and the regimentation of the corporate world or the office politics or

---

[1] Running any service business is demanding. Consultancy is more demanding than most service businesses because of the typical difficulty of the problems that consultants are normally involved with. IT consultancy business offers an additional dimension of difficulty because of the speed with which the subject changes and the fact that quite a lot of IT consultancy involves in some way the management of change which is notoriously problematic.

because you didn't see how you would be promoted under your current circumstances you may be happy to sustain a low level of business activity and not be too bothered by growth. Of course if you got into this business because you felt that you were going to have lashings of free time to pursue your numerous interests and hobbies you will probably already have made a flop of it and will have since gone back to finding a job and you will probably be as miserable in your new work as you were before. Going into business on your own, whether it is in IT consultancy or any other business activity, in order to have more free time is not likely to succeed. Starting up a new business is an extraordinarily time consuming business especially in the early years. Those who think they can create a new business without a lot of effort are in for a shock.

12.3 Money versus quality of life

If you are highly entrepreneurial you will be looking to optimize your financial return at least in the medium term, on the other hand if you are more concerned with job satisfaction your interests will not be so financially oriented, but you will want to ensure a continuous flow of work that will reward you both from an interest point of view as well as from a financial perspective. A highly entrepreneurial approach will mean that you will aim for as many clients as possible – you will take on any job for which you can vaguely claim to have competence; you will employ as many people as you need and you will be largely concerned about keeping them fully employed at as high a charge-out rate as you can. You will spend much of your time worrying about the profit and loss and the cash flow. You will want to build your own head office as soon as you can and will always be mindful of taking your company to the stock market. On the other hand, pursuing a quality of the work orientation[2] will mean a much more reflective approach where you will be more selective about the work you will accept. You will not recruit many new people and you will probably obtain more hands when you need them through outsourcing or strategic alliances. Of course the profit and loss and the cash flow will still be important, but they will not be the sole or the overwhelming important driver of your business. You will probably still be working from home and enjoying

---

[2] The work orientation does not mean that you can do without any degree of financial nous or an underdeveloped sense of entrepreneurship. The point is that the quality of work and the quality of life in general will be regarded as more important than the bank balance and this will be reflected in how this type of IT consultancy business will be managed.

not having to undertake the daily commute. The idea of a head office will be anathema and although you might sell your business if you could, and the price was right, you would never want to take it to the stock market.

If you fall into the first category – the highly entrepreneurial approach – you will be looking for a return for your efforts of hundreds or thousands or million of pounds; if you are in the second category – quality of the work approach – you will be very much more modest in your financial expectations. It is important to keep this in mind because if you are highly entrepreneurial and your IT consultancy business is not making the type of money you aim to get out of it, you have to sell the business or arrange for a management buyout or wind it up or just give it away and start up another new business, which might give you the returns you require. At the end of the day business needs to be quite unsentimental especially if you have high financial expectations. The decision is simply a question of opportunity costs. You just don't stick for too long with an investment that is not making the return you are aiming at. It is your business and you will sometimes have to make tough decisions.

WHEN IT IS THE QUALITY OF THE WORK THAT IS YOUR PRIMARY DRIVER . . .

When it is the quality of the work that is your primary driver you may still have to sell up or close down if your business isn't making the type of money that will sustain your operation or your lifestyle. If your revenue is very low then you will go broke and it will be obvious that you will have to close down and find a job. But sometimes the revenue earned is just barely enough to keep going, but not really enough to be giving you a satisfactory lifestyle. Under these circumstances it can be a very tough decision to quit. But you may well have to. Again it's your business and tough decisions are part of the reality of being in charge.

While your business is functioning and whether you are driven by the entrepreneurial urge or the quality of work and life motive, there are a number of common issues which you will have to think about and address if you intend your business to continue to exist into the medium to long term. These come under four main headings:

1 Nurturing a sustainable client relationship
2 Internal administration
3 Creating a sustainable working regime
4 Seeing new opportunities

12.4 Nurturing a sustainable client relationship

There are of course exceptions but, by and large, a considerable amount of IT consultancy tends to come in rather short-term assignments from a considerable variety of clients. Thus relationships with clients are inclined to be rather short, with the consultant no longer being required when the specific job is completed.

THUS RELATIONSHIPS WITH CLIENTS ARE INCLINED TO BE RATHER SHORT . . .

It is perhaps for this reason that it is sometimes said, rather controversially, that in IT consulting it is actually impossible to nurture a really sustainable relationship with a client. Although in some sense there might be some truth in this it is certainly the case that some client relationships are more enduring than others. IT consulting assignments are often only weeks and months in length but some consultants manage to be invited back by their clients again and again over a period of many years. In this sense they have nurtured a sustainable relationship with their clients.

In Yorkshire they have a saying that there is 'nowt so queer as folk'. The IT consultant could do worse than translate this into 'nowt so queer as clients'. The relationship between the IT consultant and the client can be quite difficult or even tricky. You will be aware that there are numerous jokes about consultants which point out how inadequate their assistance can be or how they take advantage of their clients. Consultants are often employed as a sort of last resort. They are sometimes resented by substantial numbers of the client's staff[3] because they are perceived to be costing a lot of money and sometimes the organization may not be able to point precisely to the value they are bringing to the business. By the way when this occurs it is often as much the fault of the company as it is that of the consultant.

12.4.1 IT consultants are offered jobs

IT consultants are used by organizations for multiple reasons. Sometimes consultants are employed to do things that the

---

[3] It was recently pointed out that consultants were being used in some companies to take on work that would normally have been done by full-time permanent staff and that this has sometimes caused a degree of resentment from those who perceive the consultants being used instead of the company creating more internal job opportunities.

organization does not have the resources to do. Either their own staff are too busy with their current commitments or perhaps they do not think they will have a sustainable need for the skill set currently required. IT consultants are sometimes employed to give an opinion and make a recommendation. This may be on a subject about which there is some uncertainty in the organization or it may in fact be to obtain a confirmatory opinion and make a recommendation that supports the management view. This latter approach to the use of consultants can be to try to deflect the reaction to bad news away from the senior management and onto the outsiders who will shortly after the report has been absorbed simply go away to their next assignment.

In general IT consultants find that clients do not sign up for long periods. If the client needs you for a long period he or she will almost certainly offer you a job. As an IT consultant being offered a full-time permanent job again can be very flattering. And if your IT consulting business is not doing too well you may wish to give such an offer serious consideration. However, if you are tempted to take such an offer, make sure that you recall the reasons why you previously gave up your last full-time permanent job and be reasonably sure that you won't in a matter of weeks or months feel the same way about this new job opportunity as you did about your last employment.[4]

Nurturing as sustainable a relationship with a client as possible usually involves getting to know both the organization in which you are working and the individuals involved. It also requires you to understand where the organization wants to go. Your challenge is to be able to find ways in which you can support the organization's endeavours. There is also the need for you to be prepared to offer support to the organization as seamlessly as possible. This probably means your being available on short notice to meet difficult deadlines. What this amounts to in short is that the IT consultant needs to be as flexible and as available as possible. It needs to be made clear that the work performed by the consultant is value for money. Value for money is a central issue for all IT consultants. If the client feels that he or she is getting value for money the relationship is likely to be sustainable, on the other hand if the client for any reason comes to believe that he or she is not then there are problems ahead.

---

[4] IT consultants do get offered great jobs but many have felt the return to the hierarchy and the bureaucracy of a large organization to be quite difficult after the different type of working conditions they have while working for themselves.

When the client accepts that value for money is being delivered then this will tend to nurture the consultant's relationship with the client. But as a consultant you should be aware that there are no guarantees of work continuity. It is a never-ending task to keep clients impressed with what you are doing for them and for the vast majority of consultants assignments will come to an end and they will just have to move on to another opportunity.

12.5 Internal administration

The internal administration is how you keep control of what you are doing by establishing a set of procedures as to how you find clients, write proposals, do the actual consulting work, bill clients, calculate and pay your VAT, collect money, lodge your tax returns pay yourself and your staff, etc.

In a small start-up IT consultancy business these need not be too onerous. However, they are really very important because if you do not have an ordered approach to your internal administration you can easily find yourself tripping over your own tracks with your clients and prospects and looking quite unprofessional. If you do not have an ordered approach to your invoicing your cash flow can get out of control and you can end up in financial difficulty. If your company returns are not kept up to date you can find yourself in trouble with the authorities or with your bank or with your staff if you, for example, unexpectedly run out of cash with which to pay them.

The cost of ensuring that your internal administration is in good order is not material to an even moderately successful IT consulting business, but the cost of not keeping good order can be catastrophic.

... DETAILED RECORDS OF CLIENTS AND PROSPECT CONTACTS

Key points to look out for include:

1 Keeping detailed records of client and prospect contacts.
2 Writing clear proposals for work and following these proposals up in a timely and consistent way.
3 Making sure that your terms and conditions of business are clear when you discuss possible work opportunities with prospective clients.

4 Ensuring that your have a contract or at least a letter of agreement for the work you are doing or about to undertake.

5 Agree an unambiguous understanding of exactly what the deliverables are and when you are required to produce them.

6 Having a clear understanding of when you will be paid. Will you have an early payment discount? Do you want to be paid directly into your bank account or do you want to receive a cheque?

7 If you are being paid by cheque make sure that your incoming cheques are banked regularly.

8 Making sure that your banking arrangements are efficient and effective. Banks can be very unsympathetic to small businesses. Ensure that all your financial obligations are met on time, especially your VAT where penalties can be severe for being late.

9 Keeping an eye on the costs of a company car and other perks.

10 Watching your profit and loss and especially your cash flow.

12.5.1 Understanding how your business is doing

Of the above list of major points to look out for, watching your profit and loss and especially your cash flow is probably the most important. If you are not earning adequate profits or if your cash flow is not steady[5] and sufficient to pay your expenses you will not survive in business for long. Thus one of your main tasks is to continually monitor your financial circumstances.

To do this you have to understand how to read a set of financial accounts. It really doesn't matter if you keep your financial accounts yourself or whether you have a professional firm of accountants or bookkeepers. But whichever way you do this you need to understand these documents so that you can interpret how your business is actually doing. This is not a difficult task, although if you have had no experience of such documents you may need to read an appropriate book or take a short course.

There are four different financial statements you need to be able to read and understand.

1 Income statements (sometimes called profit and loss accounts)
2 Cash flow statements

---

[5] Few start-up IT consulting businesses really have cash flowing inward. Irregular cash flows can of course be compensated for by bank overdrafts which are expensive and not always that easy to obtain.

3 Balance sheets

4 Funds flow statements

By far the most important of these from the point of view of managing your IT consulting business are the income statement and the cash flow statement. The information supplied in the balance sheet and the funds flow statement although very useful will not directly help to make important decisions that will typically be required in the start-up IT consulting environment.

12.5.2 Income statements

The income statements simply list all the money you have earned or at least invoiced and all the expenses you have incurred for a given period of time. An income statement is a historical document which is drawn up at the end of the business period. The difference between the total amount you have invoiced and the total of all your expenses for the period is either your overall profit (if income is higher than expenses) or your loss (if expenses are higher than income). A typical income statement is shown in Figure 12.1.

Income statement	£	£
for the year ending on 31 March 200X		
Revenue		75,000
Travel	15,000	
Proposal and report production	3,000	
Direct costs		18,000
Gross profit		57,000
Marketing services	7,000	
Rent	14,000	
Secretarial services	6,500	
Telephone, fax and e-mail	3,500	
Training and development	5,000	
Overheads		36,000
Net profit		21,000

Figure 12.1

A typical income statement for an IT consultancy

The profit (or the loss) is normally calculated in two steps. In the first place a gross profit is calculated. The gross profit is defined as the revenue which is simply the total of the invoices raised less the direct expenses incurred in doing the actual work invoiced. In an IT consultancy business there are probably only two direct expenses that are incurred and these are travel to and from the client and the preparation of the proposal and the report.

In the case of travel costs, many IT consulting contracts will include travel as a separately invoiced item as it can be a material cost to the consultant. The cost of preparing proposals and reports with desktop publishing is not the expense it used to be. However, it can still be substantial if it is reproduced to a high quality standard.

The second profit to be calculated is the net profit and this is simply the gross profit less all the other expenses such as rent, marketing, secretarial services, etc. It is on the net profit that you will be judging your business and it is also on this profit that income tax will be paid.[6]

You will need to do an income statement at least once a year for income tax and for the Companies Office, if you are working as a limited liability company. Your bank manager may also want to see your income statement periodically. However, as a tool to help you run your IT consulting business you may want to produce an income statement every quarter or even every month.

12.5.3 Cash flow statements

A cash flow statement is a forecast of when you expect to receive actual cash from your clients or other sources if you are negotiating a loan and when you will have to pay money out to your creditors, etc. Therefore all the items in the cash flow statement are assumptions. A typical cash flow statement is shown in Figure 12.2.

To be able to prepare a cash flow statement and to understand its implications it is most important to know exactly what assumptions have been made about the timing of cash receipts

---

[6] It is not the intention of this book to go into any detail concerning the tax liability faced by a successful IT consultant. It is very important for anyone who is self-employed to take professional tax advice from a qualified tax accountant or lawyer.

Cash flow statement	£	£	£	£	£	£
for the next six months						
Assumptions:						
50% paid in the month invoiced						
50% paid within 30 days						
Rent, secretarial and telephone costs paid in the month incurred						
Marketing and training and development cost paid one month later						
	April	May	June	July	Aug	Sept
Revenue invoiced	6,000	7,000	6,000	8,000	9,000	10,000
Cash receipts	3,000	6,500	6,500	7,000	8,500	9,500
Rent, secretarial and telephone	2,000	2,000	2,000	2,000	2,000	2,000
Marketing and training and development		1,000	1,000	1,000	1,000	1,000
Monthly cash balance	1,000	3,500	3,500	4,000	5,500	6,500
Cumulative cash balance	1,000	4,500	8,000	12,000	17,500	24,000

Figure 12.2
A typical cash flow statement for an IT consultancy

and payments. Therefore the assumptions need to be stated clearly at the beginning of the statement. You will notice in Figure 12.2 there are four sets of assumption stated.

Notice the amount of cash received always lags behind the amount of sales revenue that has been invoiced. In some IT consultancy businesses this can be a big problem and can even lead to bankruptcy. However, careful planning of your cash over a period of time will ensure that you have the money to pay your debts when it is required.

It is important to note that the flow of cash of a business can change quite quickly and therefore the cash flow statement may need continuous monitoring and updating. In a start-up situation you may well need to amend your cash flow statement at least monthly.

12.5.4 Balance sheets

For every business the balance sheet is the financial document that ultimately describes the financial health of the enterprise.

A balance sheet is often described as a financial photograph of a business at a particular moment in time. Thus the balance sheet is always declared to be at or on a definite date. The balance sheet lists all the assets that the business owns and all the different sources of funds that have been used to finance the acquisition of these assets.

It is usual to group the business's assets into two major categories. These are fixed assets and current assets. The fixed assets are those that have been bought with the intention of being used inside the business. In the case of the IT consultant the personal computer, the photocopier and other office equipment are all fixed assets as is the business motor vehicle. All these assets are bought, used by the business until they wear out or are obsolete and then they are disposed of as second-hand or used items.

On the other hand current assets are those that change form during the natural cycle of the business. In a trading business, which an IT consultancy is not, the current assets will be continually moving from cash to inventories to debtors and back to cash again. In the case of the IT consultancy the current assets will usually be only debtors and cash and sometimes some prepaid expenses. Of course if some kind of product is acquired as was described in Chapter 9 then there may be an inventory item in current assets as well.

A typical balance sheet is shown in Figure 12.3.

Besides the detailing of the business's assets a balance sheet will also show the sources of funds that have been used to acquire the assets – both the fixed assets and the currents.

In general there are only two sources of funds available to a business. These are funds that have been put into the business by its owners and which are referred to as owner's equity or there is money that has been borrowed which is sometimes referred to as debt or liabilities.

Within the category of funds called owner's equity there are two items. The first of these is money put directly into the business in the form of cash or perhaps in the form of equipment that is often done at the time the business is started up. If the business is being operated as a limited liability company this may be reflected as share capital or it may be simply entered in the books of account as a director's loan. The second part of owner's equity is the part of the profit that the business had earned and

Balance sheet	£	£
on 31 March 200X		
Fixed assets		25,000
Computer equipment – office and laptop	5,000	
Other office equipment	1,000	
Motor vehicle	19,000	
Current assets		13,000
Debtors	7,500	
Deposits and prepaid expenses	500	
Cash at bank	5,000	
Current liabilities		3,000
Trade creditors	2,500	
Overdraft	500	
Working capital		10,000
Owner's equity		35,000

Figure 12.3
A typical balance sheet for an IT consultancy

which has not been withdrawn by the owner or owners. This is referred to as the retained earnings.

With regards to the balance sheet item called debt or liabilities there are once again two categories. The first is long-term debt and the second is current (in effect short-term) liabilities. Current liabilities are defined as those that need to be repaid within a short period of time. The maximum period of time usually applied to this is normally one year. Long-term debt represents funds that only need to be repaid sometime in the future in excess of one year.

It is very unlikely that a start-up IT consultancy business will have much if any long-term debt. However, there may well be several different types of current liabilities the most usual of which are trade creditors, bank overdrafts and prepaid fees.

In presenting a balance sheet it is customary to highlight the business's working capital. The working capital is defined as the difference between the current assets and current liabilities and it is generally regarded as a measure of the business's liquidity. If the working capital is a positive number the business is probably able to pay its way. If the working capital is negative the business will usually be in trouble and it may not have sufficient liquid funds to pay its bills on time.[7]

12.5.5 Funds flow statements

The fourth financial document, that the IT consultant needs to be familiar with is the funds flow statements.[8] A funds flow statement shows how money has been used during the last business period. The way the funds flow statement is calculated is to take two consecutive balance sheets and to subtract the figures item by item from both documents. This is shown in Figure 12.4.

Thus in the funds flow statement the value of the fixed assets from the current period has the value of the fixed assets from the previous period subtracted and the resulting figure shows by how much the fixed assets have either increased or decreased in the period under review. In Figure 12.4 this business has spent an additional £5,000 on fixed assets. Similarly it has increased the current assets by £3,000. Then there has been an increase of £8,000 used by the business across these two areas. This £8,000 has been funded by an increase in liabilities, specifically an increase of £2,000 from current liabilities and an increase in owner's equity in the sum of £6,000.

The value of the funds flow statement is that it shows how money is being used or invested in the business and what sources of funds are being employed to supply these monies. The IT consultant needs to review this funds flow statement at least once a year.

---

[7] This is a very simplified analysis of business liquidity and the IT consultant will rapidly have to learn a lot more about this subject if he or she is to survive in business. However, it is beyond the scope of this book to engage in a full discussion of financial ratio analysis.

[8] The funds flow statement is also called the source and application of funds account.

Funds flow statement	31 March 200X–1	31 March 200X	Funds flow
on 31 March 200X	£	£	£
Fixed assets	20,000	25,000	5,000
Computer equipment – office and laptop			
Other office equipment			
Motor vehicle			
Current assets	10,000	13,000	3,000
Debtors			
Deposits and prepaid expenses			
Cash at bank			
Current liabilities	1,000	3,000	2,000
Trade creditors			
Overdraft			
Owner's equity	29,000	35,000	6,000

Figure 12.4
A typical funds flow statement for an IT consultancy

12.6 Creating a sustainable working regime

Being your own boss offers you great challenges and opportunities. It can also offer a type of freedom, but is often a surprise to those who are thinking about going on their own to realize that it usually means working much harder and longer hours than you have ever done before. In a full-time permanent job there are always some rules with regards to hours of work. It is true that in recent years employers have expected longer working days from their staff and have had at least sometimes no compunction in asking staff to work on the weekends. But there has always been either some explicitly recognized limit or at least some implicit recognition of when enough has been asked.

139

When you are self-employed there is often no one to keep in check the amount of time you can work. It is really down to you. Some IT consultants will work every day of the year and will put in as much as 18 hours per day. There need not be anything intrinsically wrong with this, but it certainly is not recommended if some sort of balanced life is sought. And of course there is also the question of sustainability and the quality of the output under such circumstances.

It is probably useful for you to give some thought to the issue of working commitment before getting going on your own. Questions you need to ask include:

1 How many hours per week do you need to work?
2 How many weeks a year vacation will you take?
3 How long do you think your working life will be, i.e. when do you want to retire?
4 What do you expect to do about your pension?
5 How will you handle being ill?
6 When do you engage your first employee and should this be another consultant?
7 When do you need to look for a partner?

12.6.1 How many hours per week do you need to work?

There is no doubt that the number of hours a week that you will work will be quite variable. However, it is unlikely that you will be able to achieve as much as you need to in a 40 hour week. In the first year or two you will probably find yourself working a 50 or 60 or even 70 hour week. However, except in very exceptional circumstances it is really quite difficult to sustain this level of effort and you will probably find that over the first few years you may well reduce the initial amount of time you are spending on this work.

12.6.2 How many weeks a year vacation will you take?

You may well find it difficult to find the time to take four weeks a year vacation. In the early years of your IT consultancy business you may find it necessary to reduce this to one or two weeks. Certainly it is not easy to take a four-week period off without impacting your work schedule. Of course if your business is not doing well then there may be more opportunity to take leave, but this will probably be a sign that your business venture will not survive in the long term.

12.6.3 How long do you think your working life will be, i.e. when do you want to retire?

In the circumstances of self-employment the question of retirement becomes one of when do you expect to make enough money to be financially independent? This in turn begs the question of how much money do you *need* to be financially independent and the answer to this question is the same as the proverbial 'How long is a piece of string?'

In general IT consultancy is a tough business and many practitioners will not want to carry on with this profession into old age. On the other hand for those who would find the thought of retirement unattractive, being self-employed means that you decide when you want to stop working, or indeed reduce the workload. Certainly there are management and IT consultants working into their seventies.

12.6.4 What do you expect to do about your pension?

If you make a great success of your IT consulting business you may end up either selling or floating it on the stock market. In either case you will have plenty of cash to provide for your old age.

SICK, TIRED, OLD IT CONSULTANT. PLEASE HELP.

. . . YOU WILL NEED TO CREATE A PENSION FUND FOR YOURSELF

On the other hand there are many IT consultants who have a perfectly satisfactory business and never achieve such success. These businesses just make a good living for their proprietors year after year. If this is how your business turns out you will need to create a pension fund for yourself. There are numerous ways of doing this and there are many pension advisers who will provide competent advice to you.

12.6.5 How will you handle being ill?

Falling ill is a major problem for anyone who is self-employed. There are really only two ways to cope which this situation. The first is to move to having staff or a partner to take on your responsibilities while you are away incapacitated. The second is to acquire insurance, which will cover you to some extent during a period of illness. However, insurance payout may not be too substantial and staff and partners may not be able to hold the situation for too long. There is not very much you can do in these circumstances and thus your health needs to be a consideration when you are deciding on whether to go into business on your own. In simple terms a serious illness can seriously disrupt your business as it can also disrupt your career.

12.6.6 When do you engage your first employee and should this be another consultant?

The question of when you engage your first employee is of course a function of the amount of business you have been able to attract. As soon as your cash flow justifies it you should consider what help would improve your ability to manage your business better. This could be a question of having some administrative and secretarial help, but it could also be useful to have another consultant if you can find enough work for him or her. The problem of course is to be able to sustain this work and there is no easy way of knowing when you will have reached such a position. This will essentially be a question of attempting to secure a contract or contracts from your more important clients.

Do bear in mind, as soon as you acquire staff the nature of what you are doing will change. Up to that point all you will have had to do is to act as an IT consultant and manage your own time. Now you will have to do both of these things and manage someone else's time too.

It should be borne in mind that if you are working from home there may be problems in employing a member of staff in terms of local council or municipal regulations and these need to be checked. If this is the case then you may have to move to an office or you may be able to cope by acquiring help on a freelance basis. In the latter case the individuals concerned would effectively be working for you, but based in their own homes. You will be creating your own virtual organization and taking an outsourcing route to this.

12.6.7 When do you need to look for a partner?

It is sometimes quite difficult for a small start-up IT consultancy business to find staff, especially additional, suitably qualified consultants, and it may be necessary to offer those who join you a partnership or at least a potential partnership. This of course should not be done lightly as it will have long-term implications. It is often much harder to get out of such an agreement than to create them. It is sometimes thought that you could sell a share to an incoming partner and if this is the case the longer you keep the whole business to yourself the more valuable it may be. But always remember that you will share your success and failures with your partner and that you can end up being liable for his or her mistakes. In general the question of taking on a partner needs to be answered with considerable reflection.

12.7 Seeing new opportunities

No aspect of business is ever static for long. By the very nature of business products, services, public attitudes and needs, economies and markets are always continuously evolving. New business with new ideas and concepts are continually being launched. It is for this reason that few businesses ever really last a long time. They go broke or they are gobbled up by other firms through mergers or acquisitions. One of the effects of this is that the average age of a firm on the stock market is said to be about 40 years. The average age of a privately held small business is probably much shorter.

If you wish to stay in business for even the medium term, say five to ten to even 20 years, then you need to manage this natural evolution for your IT consulting business. No matter how good your original business idea was it is unlikely that you will be able to sustain it as the primary driver of your business activities for more than a few years. You need to be continuously on the lookout for changes in the market and you need to be able to respond to them in a creative way and thus establish and keep a competitive advantage for yourself. Finding good business ideas is really quite tough, but it is a central part of being able to stay in business. If you cannot generate a steady flow of good business ideas you will not survive. There is no formula for doing this. It is the central characteristic of being an entrepreneur. And of course a good business idea will not always lead to a business success. The aphorism 'There's many a slip twixt the cup and the lip' is appropriate here. Having your own business just means being interested in all things that go on around you and looking at them with creative business eyes. It is a habit you will need to cultivate right from the very beginning.

143

IF YOU ARE SUFFICIENTLY ADAPTABLE AND A LITTLE
LUCKY YOUR BUSINESS SHOULD PROSPER AND GROW

If you are sufficiently adaptable and a little lucky your business should prosper and grow. Within a few years you may well be employing several other consultants and perhaps using other consulting resources through outsourcing arrangements. There is no reason why you could not develop over a five to 10 year period a very prosperous business that could have substantial market value.

On the way to this success you will quite possibly want to acquire your own corporate head office. This need not be a very big affair as there are plenty of business parks in which you can acquire excellent medium scale business accommodation. You can buy, rent or lease these. However, you need to be confident that you do really have a strong business with sufficient appeal to its client base to stay in business for quite some time.[9]

During this period you may well be approached to see if your business is for sale. Most entrepreneurs would say that their business is always for sale, but at the right price. You might also take that attitude. However, it may well be a mistake to sell your business too early.[10] If you are on a growth streak then you need to carefully consider whether to take the money and think about doing something else or growing the business further and perhaps end up with a much bigger sum. Of course growth streaks do run out and even the most successful businesses do find themselves in the doldrums from time to time.

As well as being made offers to sell your business you will also find that you will be invited to buy other businesses and or to invest in other enterprises. Sometimes these suggestions concern enterprises that are complementary to your own business and

[9] Before putting money into a corporate head office make sure that you really can afford it. Also make sure that you are doing this for the right reasons. Clients are often indifferent about their IT consultants' premises. More and more IT consultancies are asking their workers to be based from home and to go directly to the client's premises. So there is not all that much need for expensive corporate head office accommodation any more.

[10] The proprietor of a successful IT consultancy business will frequently receive enquiries as to whether the business is for sale. However, these will frequently be nothing more than fishing expeditions by those who are seeking to find a cheap business for sale. The problem is that a lot of time can be wasted on these enquiries so you should really decide if it is the right time to sell and make sure that your enquirer is really serious.

there may well be merit in them. However, many such offers will be in activities that are not that close to what you have set out to do and it is really important not to dilute your focus from the main event. Sticking to your knitting is an important precept when setting up and developing your own IT consultancy business.

There are very few IT consultancies that have been successful enough to be taken to the stock market. But with the amazing stock market behaviour over the past few years this might turn out to be a possible opportunity if you end up with a successful business.

There is no doubt that managing or minding your own business is a challenge, but it is a very rewarding one which if you are successful will bring with it much pleasure and many rewards.

12.7.1 Growing from strength to strength

Even from the early days of your IT consulting business just your administrative work may take you as much as half an hour per day. Once your business grows a bit this can easily grow into half a day a week. Although this may not at first sound much, when you consider that you need to make sure your current clients are fully attended to and that you still have to keep an eye on where you are going to find your next client, the time required for administration becomes a burden. It is therefore important to find help and to set up procedures for coping with this work. Administrative work is always important but it is seldom urgent (except for invoicing promptly) and thus it can often be left to the last minute and thus degenerate into a crisis. This should not be allowed to happen. It is thus important if you are to grow your business successfully to set this up carefully with a part-time bookkeeper or administrator. Eventually your IT consultancy may grow sufficiently to need a full-time person and increased office space but this will probably be sometime in the future.

You may find that your IT consultancy business may not grow smoothly. Very often you will encounter periods of quite fast growth where you will be rushed off your feet and this may be followed by periods that are essentially quiet. The problem then is the balancing of demand and supply. If you expand your business to cope with a temporary surge in demand you may well find that you will have to downsize once this demand has returned to what was probably normal. Downsizing is never easy and is often quite unpleasant. Sometimes it is just not possible, as is the case if you have, on a surge of enthusiasm for your business growth, signed up a long lease on a property. This can actually lead to your business failing. In general being able to detect a permanent shift in the level of your business activity is a crucial factor in successfully growing your business. If you can't develop a feel for this then you will be a victim of continuous swings and endless expansion and contraction.

In a similar way it is a major challenge for you to know if you should increase your own take home pay or acquire a bigger or better company car. To survive in the IT consultancy business you need to ensure that you have an adequate level of reserves that will see you through any short- to medium-term downturn or contraction in your business. It is not possible to speculate as to how much this should be for any particular business circumstance but it should always be a question of having at least several months' expenses available. Once this has been secured then it is optimal if you want to take a bigger share of the profits from the business in any form that you wish.

With a prudent approach to theses issues and a little bit of luck your IT consultancy should grow from strength to strength.

12.7.2 What the Internet can do for you

As a general directory and information accessing tool the Internet can really assist the IT consultant in obtaining facts and figures about the various services he or she will need to manage the business. There are many websites that give useful information about tax, VAT, etc. See http://www.ukonline.gov.uk as a gateway for this.

There are a number of discussion groups and forums that the IT consultant can participate in. These might be linked to the industry your clients are working in or they might be communities for other IT consultants in which you can discuss issues of common interest. See for example, http://groups.google.com/groups?hl=en&group=uk.consultants. All the major search engines run groups and these can be searched to find topics of interest.

12.8 Summary and conclusion

It is not a trivial business to start an IT consultancy business but it is much more difficult to sustain one over a period of time. To succeed at this it takes a lot of hard work and much dedication.

There are many things to do and to get right. It is very hard if not impossible for an IT consultant to do all of these on his or her own. There is no doubt that you will need help. So before you start make sure that you have at least identified the sources of help that you can call up when you need them.

An IT consultancy business will not usually mushroom overnight or for that matter in a few weeks or a few months. You may have to keep working hard with only modest success for at least several months and maybe even years before the business will flourish. Therefore it is really important not to give up too soon. Just keep at it. In IT consultancy perseverance is often well rewarded with very handsome results.

12.9 Checklist

Things to think about when minding your own business

1 How well is your IT consulting business getting on? Are you meeting the objectives you had when you set yourself up in business?

2 Have you established good relationships with your current clients? How long do you expect to obtain business from them?

3 Are you flexible and adaptive enough to be able to pick up any opportunity that your clients may offer to you?

4 Have you been good at coming up with new ideas to sell to your clients and prospective clients? How many new ideas have you come up with in the past few months?

5 Have you got a reasonable sales monitoring and management system in place? Do you know whom you have sent proposals to on what issues and how they have been followed up? Do you have a systematic approach to keeping in touch with your past clients and your prospective clients?

6 Are your terms and conditions of business quite clear? Do you have a form of contract for your clients?

7 Do you have suitable accounting/administrative procedures and controls in place? Have you adequate help with you accounting, VAT returns, etc.

8 Do you know if you are making profit? Have you enough cash to meet your outgoings for the next few months?

9 What is your policy towards working conditions for yourself and for your employees if you have any? Have you made

adequate provision for the possibility of being ill, etc.? Have you made arrangements for a pension fund?

10 Are you open to new opportunities concerning employing extra staff or entering partnerships or joining a strategic alliance, etc.?

11 How would you go about looking at a new opportunity in a similar or complementary business?

12 How would you go about downsizing your operation if your business activity took a downturn?

Useful magazines and journals

Business Week
http://www.businessweek.com

BYTE
www.BYTE.com

Computer Weekly
Quadrant House, The Quadrant, Sutton
Tel: 020 8652 8642
www.cw360.com
e-mail: computer.weekly@rbi.co.uk

Computing
32–34 Broadwick Street, London W1A 2HG
Tel: 020 7316 9000
http://www.computing-media.co.uk

Consultants' Advisory
PMP UK Limited, Witton House, Lower Road, Chorleywood,
Hertfordshire WD3 5LB
Tel: 01923 285323
http://www.consultants-advisory.com.

Contract Professional
guide for IT contractors and consultants

The Economist
www.Economist.com

EWeek
(formerly PC Week), news and features covering developments in the computer industry

Information Age
Elan European Publishing Ltd, 12 Dyott Street, London WC1A 1DF
informationage@whitaker.co.uk

Internet Business
Haymarket Publishing, 174 Hammersmith Road, London W6 7JP
www.ibmag.co.uk

IT Consultant Magazine
Hillgate Communications,
4th floor, 61 Southwark St, London SE1 0HL
Tel: 0207 620 0001
http://www.hillgate.co.uk

Journal of Management Consulting
http://www.c2m.com/

Knowledge Management
Bizmedia Ltd, 80/82 Chiswick High Road, London W4 1SY
Tel: 0118 9602820
www.kmmag.co.uk

MIND
Microsoft Interactive Developer Magazine

Mind Your Own Business Magazine
Market Place Publishing, Scorpio House, 106 Church Road, London SE19
Tel: 020 8771 3614
http://www.mindyourownbusiness.net/

Useful book list

1 Fiona Czerniawska (2000) *Management Consulting in the 21st Century*,
2 Timothy Clark, *Managing Consultants: Consultancy as the Management of Impressions (A Managing Work and Organizations)*,
3 Philip Sadler, *Management Consultancy*, 2nd Edition
4 A. Simon (1998) *How to be a Successful Computer Consultant*, McGraw-Hill, New York

5 David H. Maister (1997) *Managing the Professional Service Firm*, Free Press Paperbacks, New York

6 David H. Maister (2000) *True Professionalism*, Simon and Schuster, London

7 Michael Powell (1999) *Considering Computer Contracting? How to Become a Freelance Computer Professional*, Butterworth-Heinemann, Oxford

8 Dan Remenyi (1999) *Stop IT Project Failures Through Risk Management*, Butterworth-Heinemann, Oxford

9 Mick Cope (2000) *The Seven Cs of Consulting: Your Complete Blueprint for any Consulting Assignment*, Pearson Education, London

10 Andrew K. Johnston (1999) *A Hacker's Guide to Project Management*, Butterworth-Heinemann, Oxford

11 David M. Shailer (2001) *The Project Manager's Toolkit*, Butterworth-Heinemann, Oxford

12 Subir Chowdhury (2000) *Management 21C*, Pearson Education Ltd, London

13 *Getting Started: How to Set up your Own Business*, Robson Rhodes, Chartered Accountants, Kogan Page, 4th edition, 1995

14 D. Remenyi, M. Sherwood-Smith with Terry White (1997) *Achieving Maximum Value from your Information Systems – A Process Approach*, John Wiley and Sons, Chichester.

Useful professional associations

The British Chambers of Commerce
Manning House, 22 Carlisle Place, London SW1P 1JA
Tel: 020 7565 2000
http://www.britishchambers.org.uk

British Computer Society
1 Sanford Street, Swindon, Wiltshire SN1 1HJ
Tel: +44 (0) 1793 417424
http://www.bcs.org.uk

British Consultants Bureau
One Westminster Palace Gardens, Artillery Row,
London SW1P 1RJ
Tel: 020 7222 3651
http://www.bcb.co.uk

British Venture Capital Association
Essex House, 12–13, Essex Street, London WC2R 3AA
Tel: 020 7240 3846
http://www.bvca.co.uk

**Central Computer and Telecommunications Agency (CCTA)
and Office of Government Commerce**
Rosebery Court, St Andrew's Business Park, Norwich,
Norfolk NR7 0HS
Tel: 0845 000 4 999. International callers please dial
(+44) 845 000 4999
http://www.ogc.gov.uk/ogc/ogc.help.nsf/pages/redirect.html

Chartered Institute of Management Accounts
26 Chapter Street, London SW1P 4NP
Tel: +44 (0) 20 7663 5441
http://www.cima.org.uk

Chartered Institute of Marketing
Moor Hall, Cookham, Maidenhead, Berkshire SL6 9QH
Tel: +44 (0) 1628 427500
http://www.cim.co.uk

Chartered Institute of Taxation
12 Upper Belgrave Street, London SW1X 8BB
Tel: 020 7235 9381
http://www.tax.org.uk

Computing Services and Software Association
20 Red Lion Street, London WC1R 4QN
Tel: 020 7395 6700
http://www.cssa.co.uk

Electronic Commerce Association (ECA)
e.centre, 10 Maltravers Street, London
WC2R 3BX
Tel: 020 7655 9000
http://www.eca.org.uk/

**Information Technology National Training Organization
(ITNTO)**
e-skills NTO, 1 Castle Lane, London SW1E 6DR
Tel: 020 7963 8920
http://www.e-skillsnto.org.uk/

Institute of Chartered Accountants in England and Wales
Chartered Accountants' Hall, PO Box 433, London EC2P 2BJ
Tel: 020 7920 8100
http://www.icaew.co.uk

Institute of Chartered Accountants of Scotland
27 Queen Street, Edinburgh EH2 1LA
Tel: 0131 225 5673
http://www.icas.org.uk

Institute of Directors
116 Pall Mall, London SW1Y 5ED
Tel: 020 7839 1233
http://www.iod.com

Institute of IT Training
Institute House, University of Warwick Science Park,
Coventry CV4 7EZ
Tel: +44 (0) 24 7641 8128
http://www.iitt.org.uk/

Institute of Management
Management House, Cottingham Road, Corby,
Northamptonshire NN17 1TT
Tel: +44 (0) 1536 204222
http://www.inst-mgt.org.uk/

Institute of Management Consultants
3rd floor, 17–18 Hayward's Place, London EC1R 0EQ
Tel: 020 7566 5220
http://www.imc.co.uk/

Institute for the Management of Information Systems (IMIS)
5 Kingfisher House, New Mill Road, Orpington,
Kent BR5 3QG
Tel: +44 (0) 700 00 23456
http://www.imis.org.uk/

The Institution of Analysts and Programmers
Charles House, 36 Culmington Road, London W13 9NH
Tel: +44 (0) 20 8567 2118
http://www.iap.org.uk/

Institution of Electrical Engineers (IEE)
IEE, Savoy Place, London WC2R 0BL
http://www.iee.org/

International Federation for Information Processing
Hofstraße 3,
A-2361 Laxenburg, Austria
Tel: +43 2236 73616
http://www.ifip.or.at/

Management Consultancies Association
11 West Halkin Street, London SW1X 8JL
Tel: 020 7235 3897
http://www.mca.org.uk

The National Association of Round Tables of Great Britain and Ireland
Marchesi House, 4 Embassy Drive, Calthorpe Road,
Edgbaston, Birmingham B15 1TP
Tel: +44 (0) 121 456 4402
http://www.roundtable.org.uk/

Rotary Club of Great Britain
Kinwarton Road, Alcester, Warwickshire B49 6BP
Tel: 01789 765 411
http://www.ribi.org/

Training courses and opportunities

Academy Internet
e-Business training and e-learning solutions
http://www.academyinternet.com

Chameleon Training
Offers range of training opportunities
http://www.chameleontraining.co.uk

European Computer Driving Licence
IT skills training
http://www.ecdl.com/

Information Technology National Training Organization (ITNTO)
http://www.e-skillsnto.org.uk/

Price Waterhouse
Courses available
http://www.pwcglobal.com/uk/eng/car-inexp/graduate/mcs/courses/.html

Useful software

The software listed here is in addition to the standard office tools such as e-mail, word processing, spreadsheet, etc. that will be required.

Browse3d
Software that lets you see up to 16 websites simultaneously on the screen
http://www.browse3d.com

Mind Your Own Business
Software to manage a small business
http://www.myob.co.uk/

Quicken
http://www.quicken.com

SAGE Accounting Software
http://www.sage.com

Microsoft Project
http://www.microsoft.com/office/project/default.asp

TheBrain
Software to manage your computer filing system
http://www.thebrain.com

Note that all Web addresses are valid at the time of going to press, but will no doubt change in time.

Useful search engines

http://inktomi.com
http://search.aol.com
http://search.msn.com
http://search.netscape.com
http://www.alltheweb.com
http://www.altavista.com
http://www.ask.com
http://www.directhit.com
http://www.excite.com
http://www.google.com
http://www.hotbot.com
http://www.iwon.com
http://www.looksmart.com
http://www.lycos.com
http://www.mamma.com
http://www.overture.com
http://www.webcrawler.com
http://www.yahoo.com

Ezines and newsletters

Lists of Ezines by category

CMPnet
Popular news site
http://www.cmpnet.com

Connect Web Magazine
http://www.connectweb.co.uk

E Business Advisor Magazine
http://www.advisor.com

Ezines
www.compinfo-center.com/itmags/htm
Site showing computer publications and Ezines
and
http://bestezines.com/ezines/business.htm

Fast Company
http://www.fastcompany.com

Integrated Solutions Magazine
http://www.integratedsolutionsmag.com/Recent.htm

Internet World
Coverage of Internet technologies, e-commerce and online
marketing, ISP resources and Web development.
http://www.iw.com/

IT Consultant
http://www.hillgate.co.uk

Itworld.com
Newsletters offering industry news, technology updates, etc.
http://www/itworld.com

Management Consultancy
http://www.managementconsultancy.co.uk

Management Consultant Decisions International
http://www.sterlingpublications.com/publications/
mgmtconsultdecisions.html

Management Consultant News
http://www.pmp.co.uk

**National Market Reports and Management Consulting
Newsletter**
http://www.alpha-publications.com

Red Herring
The business of technology
http://www.redherring.com

Upside Today
The Tech Insider
http://www.upsidetoday.com/

vnunet.com
UK technical news, reviews and downloads
http://www.vnunet.com

Wired News
Background stories of successful Internet businesses, trends
and visions of the online world
http://www.wired.com

ZdNet
http://www.techupdate.zdNet.com

Interesting websites

http://eevl.icbl.hw.ac.uk/
Internet guide to engineering, mathematics and computing

http://www.bexa.co.uk
British Exporters Association

http://www.bl.uk/
British Library

http://www.britishcouncil.com
The British Council

http://www.business-directory-uk.co.uk
UK business directory

http://www.companieshouse.gov.uk
Companies House

http://www.dma.org.uk
Marketing Association (UK)

http://www.dpr.gov.uk/
Data Protection Register

http://www.elance.com
Bid for projects in the market place

http://www.enterprise-centre.co.uk

http://www.eurim.org/
All-party, pan-industry 'lobby' where the politics of the information society and e-commerce are discussed across political,
organizational and national boundaries prior to public debate

http://www.export.org.uk
Institute of Export

http://www.fsb.org.uk
Federation of Small Businesses

http://www.indusoc.co.uk
Industrial Society

http://www.morebusiness.com
A site for business plan development

http://www.ncc.co.uk
The National Computing Centre

http://www.netvalley.com
Ranks magazines by net influence

http://www.oft.gov.uk
Office of Fair Trading

http://www.patent.gov.uk
Patent Office

http://www.searchenginewatch
Excellent information source about search engines

http://www.sie.ed.ac.uk/business.htm
Scottish Institute of Enterprise – setting up your own business

http://www.sussexenterprise.co.uk/

http://www.ukishelp.co.uk/
EU funding opportunities

http://www.ukonline.gov.uk/
The UK Government portal

http://www.ukonlineforbusiness.com/
UK business portal

http://www.waller.co.uk/advice.htm
Advice on starting up a website design business

http://www.wilsonweb.com
Tips and tricks on Web marketing

Directory sites

http://www.brad.co.uk
BRAD

http://www.businesspages.co.uk
Business Pages

http://www.kellys.co.uk
KELLYS

http://www.kompass.co.uk
KOMPASS UK

http://www.thomweb.co.uk
Thomson Local Directory

Government sites

http://www.britishchambers.org.uk
http://www.btgplc.co.uk
http://www.businesslink.co.uk
http://www.bvca.co.uk
http://www.dti.gov.uk
http://www.enterprisezone.org.uk
http://www.hmce.gov.uk
http://www.inlandrevenue.gov.uk/home.htm

Chatrooms for consultants

www.deltalk.us.del
www.smallbustechtalk.com

Index

Staff:
  cooperation with, 82
  recruiting, 142
  temporary, 6
Start up capital, 23
Strategic IS planning, 49
Subcontracting to friends, 119

Target market, 72
Tax, 123
Travel costs, 28, 30
Turing, Alan, 55
Turnover, initial, 25

Understanding the market, 64

Value for money, 26, 63
  client perception, 97
Variable costs, 31

VAT, 29, 123, 131
Vendor selection, 47
Viruses, 44

Watson, Thomas, Sr, 55
Web lists, 106
Websites, 79
  setting up a, 33
Wide area networks, 43
Work breakdown schedules, 85
Working at home, 29
Working hours, 13, 14, 140
World wide web, 2
Wozniak, Steve, 56
Writing a book, 108
Writing for newspapers and
  magazines, 107

Y2K, 2